A GOD-CENTERED LIFE

A 40-Day Devotional

Dr. Steve Edge

ISBN 979-8-88943-554-9 (paperback)
ISBN 979-8-88943-555-6 (digital)

Christian Faith Publishing
832 Park Avenue
Meadville, PA 16335
www.christianfaithpublishing.com

All biblical references are from the New American Standard Bible (NASB) unless otherwise indicated.

Printed in the United States of America

For Chloee, Brayden, Ethan,
Jaxson, Kaden, and Banning

Contents

An Introduction

And He (Christ) died for all, so that they who live
might no longer live for themselves, but for Him
who died and rose again on their behalf.
—2 Corinthians 5:15

This is day 1 of a 40-day journey to living a God-centered life. This book will offer you the opportunity to spend forty days considering what it means to be truly committed to God and His plan for your life. Living for Christ rather than for ourselves is the basis to living a God-centered life. Only when He becomes the very center of our lives can we really say that we are living this way.

This 40-day journey will lead you in examining five characteristics which are the foundations for living a God-centered, Christ-centered life. These characteristics include

1. avoiding the compartmentalization of our lives,
2. trusting God,
3. spending time with God,
4. meditating on God's Word, and
5. living out the truth in our daily lives.

As we exercise these five characteristics daily, we begin to grow in our faith in Christ and position ourselves to have a more intimate relationship with Him. Each day, you will be given a scripture on which to focus and meditate. Following the passage of scripture, you will find some thoughts regarding the truths found in the passage.

And at the end of each day, you will be given an opportunity to respond to what you have learned through that passage.

In order to prepare for this 40-day journey, go ahead and make some decisions as to when you will spend daily time with God as well as where you intend to accomplish this. Bring along a notebook or journal and write down anything that God may speak to you during this time. It is my sincere desire that you will emerge from this journey with a greater intimacy with your Savior and that you will be energized to spend the rest of your life in service to Him!

First Things First
It Begins at Salvation

Jesus answered and said to him, "Truly, truly, I say to you, unless one is born again he cannot see the kingdom of God."
—John 3:3

Why do we say "born again?" Because Jesus said it! For us to live a God-centered life, we first have to be born again. This is a spiritual transaction in which you move from spiritual death to spiritual life, and it is simply a matter of prayer.

God sees our hearts. We can fool people around us, but we cannot fool God. It is God alone who judges mankind and the thoughts and intentions of our hearts. Sin has put us at enmity with God, and we are all born into this world with a sin nature, a propensity to rebel against God. But "God so loved the world that He gave us His Son." This is important because it reveals to us that even though we are sinners deserving of God's judgment, His desire is for us to be saved. Again, this is a spiritual transaction that happens between God and a person when they cry out to Him for salvation, and it is wholly necessary if one is to live a God-centered life. Consider these biblical steps in receiving salvation:

1. Acknowledging God's love for you

   For God so loved the world, that He gave His only begotten Son, that whoever believes in Him shall not perish, but have eternal life. (John 3:16)

2. Admitting your need for salvation

   For all have sinned and fall short of the glory of God. (Romans 3:23)

3. Understanding that salvation is a gift

   For the wages of sin is death, but the free gift of God is eternal life in Christ Jesus our Lord. (Romans 6:23)

4. Confessing Jesus as Lord and believing (trusting) in Him

   That if you confess with your mouth Jesus *as* Lord, and believe in your heart that God raised Him from the dead, you will be saved; for with the heart a person believes, resulting in righteousness, and with the mouth he confesses, resulting in salvation. For "Whoever will call on the name of the Lord will be saved." (Romans 10:9–10, 13)

5. Living in the power of the Holy Spirit

   Peter *said* to them, "Repent, and each of you be baptized in the name of Jesus Christ for the forgiveness of your sins; and you will receive the gift of the Holy Spirit." (Acts 2:38)

The salvation of a human soul comes by faith in what Christ has done for us on the cross. It is completely apart from works and can be received by praying and asking God for salvation. In fact, the gospel is so simple that even a child can receive it. So what do we do after praying and asking God to save us?

After receiving salvation, share you decision with someone you spiritually trust. Be baptized as a testimony to your new life in Jesus!

Then find a church where you can receive biblical training and grow in your knowledge and walk with Christ. This is the most important decision you will ever make as it affects your life now and for all eternity. Living a God-centered life is impossible without a born-again salvation experience. It really does begin at salvation. But as a child of God, you are now on the road to seeing the presence, provision, and protection of God in your daily life. Lean on Him as you seek to please Him every day!

Responding to God's Word

This is the most important decision, even more important than who you will marry, where you will live, and what career path you will pursue. Salvation is the beginning point in the Christian life. At conversion, we are now positioned in Christ and given the Holy Spirit. This allows us to overcome the world and the spiritual warfare that takes place every day.

If you have never been saved or are not sure whether you are, why not pray now, admitting your need to God and asking Him to save you on the basis of what Christ has done for you on the cross, then you will be ready to begin living a God-centered life!

Idolatry
Prioritizing Christ

If anyone comes to Me, and does not hate his own father
and mother and wife and children and brothers and sisters,
yes, and even his own life, he cannot be My disciple.
—Luke 14:26

One of the most misunderstood concepts from scripture seems to be that of idolatry. We might think of *idolatry* as worshiping some image made of wood, metal, or stone. We might convince ourselves that this kind of behavior is reserved only for people in distant lands. But in reality, idolatry is "the putting of anyone or anything ahead of God." We can think of it like this: God has a rightful place to be on the throne of our lives, but when we decide to allow someone or something to sit in His rightful place, we commit idolatry.

Now, given that definition, it is not difficult to see all of the ways in which we can commit this sin. Today's passage is a good illustration of what Jesus means when He speaks of living a God-centered, Christ-centered life. All other things have to take a back seat to our relationship with Him. Otherwise, we are simply committing idolatry. God deserves our all. If we give Him anything less, we are ignoring His instructions on how to become His disciples. Consider the relationships that Jesus says have to come *after* our relationship with Him: our relationship with our parents, with our spouse, with our children, and with our siblings. In other words, our family relationships cannot become more important than our relationship with Christ.

Sometimes we hear the sentiment *family first*. Family *is* important. In fact, it is God who designed the idea of families. But we can never allow our family to become more important than our devotion to God. Jesus says that in order to follow Him, we must "hate" our mother and father, spouse and children, and brothers and sisters. Is Jesus teaching us to hate our family members? Of course not! The Bible is full of instructions on loving our families, our neighbors, and our fellow man. What Jesus is doing is using a literary device to make a point, and it is one that we must not miss. In comparison to our relationship with Him, all other relationships must become secondary.

This has a practical application as well. Often, when God calls us to a particular place or area of service, we have to be ready to leave our current location and that might even mean leaving our families. Of course, as parents of underage children, the entire family would make the move. But later in life, as we mature into adulthood, we must be ready to leave the comfort of our families in order to be obedient to Christ. So our devotion to Him must be greater than our relationship with anyone else.

At the end of the passage, Jesus even adds that we cannot love our own lives more than Him. This also hits at the core of what it means to live a God-centered, Christ-centered life. The reality is that many people live for themselves. They pursue what they want. They construct a life that they deem successful and important. But Jesus is telling us that we cannot live for ourselves and live for Him at the same time. Either He is on the throne of our lives or we are. It really is that simple. So idolatry usually follows one of three courses:

1. Idolatry: Putting *people* in God's place

    Today's passage is a clear illustration that we are not to value earthly relationships over that of our relationship with Christ. When we love people more than God, we are putting them in the place that rightfully belongs to Him.

2.   Idolatry: Putting *material things* in God's place

In addition to people, we are not to pursue material wealth over that of pursuing a relationship with Christ. When we make the gathering of material possessions more important than fostering a living, vibrant relationship with Christ, we are putting temporal things in the place that rightfully belongs to God.

3.   Idolatry: Putting *ourselves* in God's place

Finally, we are not to live for ourselves, pursing what we desire and what we want. When we live for ourselves, we are putting ourselves on the throne of our lives, the place that rightfully belongs to God.

Prioritizing Christ means effectively avoiding a life of idolatry. When God's will for our lives becomes our greatest desire, we position ourselves to experience the most abundant, fulfilling life possible. And interestingly enough, when we prioritize Christ, we are able to love others the way that God desires for us to love. We become the best parents, spouses, children, brothers, and sisters!

Responding to God's Word

Considering today's passage, would you label yourself as an idolater? Are there relationships in your life that you have allowed to become of more value to you than your relationship with Christ? Has the pursuit of material possessions become an idol? What changes do you feel you need to make in order to prioritize your relationship with Christ above everything else?

God's Desire
Relationship, Not Religion

This people draw near with their words and honor Me with their lip service, but they remove their hearts far from Me, and their reverence for Me consists of tradition learned *by rote*.
—Isaiah 29:13

Living a God-centered life is at the core of the Christian faith. Today's passage illustrates how easy it is for people to slip into a religious mode without even the slightest devotion to or knowledge of God. The people of Israel were God's people, but something happened. They were continuing in a religious structure that they had learned from birth. They were participating in religious tradition, but what God desired from them, namely their devotion and love, was absent. They were going through the motions, yet their hearts were far from God.

The same thing is true today. It is possible to go through religious motion without salvation, without spiritual life, and without surrendering of our lives to Christ. But one thing is certain; there is no substitution for a genuine relationship with Jesus Christ. When we are saved, we move from spiritual death to spiritual life, we receive the Spirit of God, He comes and lives within us, and we experience the radical change that can only come through a genuine, authentic relationship with God. This is what saving faith is all about!

So how do we know if we are merely religious or genuinely saved? Today's passage gives us some things to look for that would indicate we are participating in mere religious motion:

1.   Empty speech

This people draw near with their words and
honor Me with their lip service.

The people had begun to honor God only with their
words. Their hearts were just not in it. If you have ever
attended a worship service in which you were physically
present yet your heart and mind were on everything but
worship, then you have probably experienced this. The
honor that these people were giving God was *only* with their
words. They were not really honoring God; rather they
were just exercising "lip service." This kind of "worship"
looks good on the outside but is empty and meaningless on
the inside. When we say all of the right things yet do not
possess a passion and desire to be closer to God, chances are
we are participating in empty, religious motion.

2.   Hearts far from God

They remove their hearts far from Me.

Notice that God is saying that it was the people who
had removed their hearts far from Him. They had made a
conscious choice to engage in meaningless, spiritual activity. In fact, it was because their hearts were not in it that
made the motion meaningless. When we observe people
participating in an activity like an athletic event but are not
playing up to their full potential, we might say something
such as "Their heart just doesn't seem to be in it today."
Interestingly enough, in an athletic event, especially if the
stakes are high, that kind of lackadaisical approach simply
isn't good enough and is often not tolerated. But when it
comes to worshiping God, do we see an even greater reason for our hearts to be in it? It is possible to be religious
but not genuinely saved. It is possible to be religious yet

spiritually dead. And it is possible to be religious without possessing eternal life. We need to honor God with our mouths, but we must always check to make sure that our hearts are in agreement.

3. Based on tradition

Their reverence for Me consists of tradition.

If someone were to ask you why you do the things you do (religiously), how would you answer them? Do you know why? There are many people today that are following a spiritual model given to them by tradition. There is nothing wrong with traditions, but we must always ask the question, "Why is it important for me to do that?" If we are participating in religious motion and do not know why, we should stop and ask whether what we are doing is biblically sound. If we don't know the *why* behind what we are doing or our approach is "We've always done it this way," then it may be time to examine ourselves to see if we are indeed in a genuine, saving relationship with Christ.

4. Mechanical structure

Their reverence for Me consists of tradition learned *by rote.*

One of the clearest indicators of empty, religious motion is repetition without the slightest thought or consideration of what is being said. Most of us can probably recite something from rote such as the "Pledge of Allegiance" or "The Lord's Prayer." It is not a bad thing to be able to put in our minds something spiritually profitable. Scripture memorization is one of the foundations for living a victorious Christian life. But when we can recite these things *mechanically* without even thinking about or contemplating what we are saying, our worship of God can become robotic at best.

What had happened to the people of Israel is that they had learned how to go through the motions, saying all of the right things with their mouths, yet their hearts were not in it. This is the problem that God had with them. Their devotion, based on traditional motion and the reciting of everything by rote, existed without a genuine relationship with the one to whom they were supposedly worshiping. Religious motion is not what God desires for us. He wants us to experience a vibrant, personal, life-changing relationship with Jesus Christ. As we move through the five characteristics of a God-centered life, we will see biblically what God has in mind for those who would surrender their lives to Him!

Responding to God's Word

Are you participating in religious motion that is mechanical or robotic without a heartfelt commitment to Christ? Have you been born again? Would you be willing to exchange your religious activity for an authentic, vibrant relationship with Jesus Christ?

CHARACTERISTIC #1

Avoiding Compartmentalization

DAY 1

A God-Centric Life

Hear, O Israel! The LORD is our God, the LORD is one! You shall love the LORD your God with all your heart and with all your soul and with all your might. These words, which I am commanding you today, shall be on your heart. You shall teach them diligently to your sons and shall talk of them when you sit in your house and when you walk by the way and when you lie down and when you rise up. You shall bind them as a sign on your hand and they shall be as frontals on your forehead. You shall write them on the doorposts of your house and on your gates.

—Deuteronomy 6:4–9

God doesn't want a part of our lives; He desires all of it! Today's passage is one that anyone raised in Judaism would know by heart. As Christians, it demonstrates God's desire to be at the center of everything we are and do. Despite this truth, it is easy to find ourselves compartmentalizing our lives. To compartmentalize is to separate the various facets of our lives into categories. We could illustrate this by drawing several rectangles or boxes on a piece of paper. In each box we could write down some area of our lives. One box could be labeled "family" while another might be "career/job." Other categories could include "finances," "hobbies/leisure," and perhaps even a box for our "spiritual life." There is naturally some overlap between the different categories, but for the most part, with compartmentalization, they remain exclusive from one another. While there may be some positive aspects to compartmentalization, it simply doesn't work for a life surrendered to Jesus Christ.

Contrast the compartmentalization of life to that of what today's passage teaches us. God wants us to acknowledge Him as the only God and desires for us to love Him with *all* of our heart. He desires to be at the center of everything that we are and do. A good illustration for this kind of life would be to draw a circle representing a wheel. At the center of the wheel is Christ. All of the other facets of our lives should revolve around Him. For a politician, this would mean that any legislation written would reflect a devotion to Christ. For the businessman, all decisions made for the company would also be God honoring. We could mention any career or job, and the result would be the same. All of our attitudes, motives, and actions should reflect Christ as Lord in our lives. Even our leisure activities should reflect a devotion to God.

When Christ is at the center of our lives, everything that we think, say, and do reflects our desire to please Him. In today's passage, God is instructing the people of Israel, and by extension all born-again believers in Jesus Christ, to have this same attitude. We are to dwell on the Word of God. It is to be on our hearts and minds. We are to instruct our children about the things of God and Christ. Day and night, the most important thing for us to remember is our relationship with God. The people of Israel were to wear reminders of God's Word on their persons. If you have ever worn a wristband with a message or scripture on it, you are doing just that! They were to put reminders of His Word in their houses. It is quite common to see this practiced today as well. We can post scriptures on our refrigerators, bathroom mirrors, or some other prominent place around the house. And all of this is for one reason. We are to live our lives with God at the center.

While compartmentalization allows us to keep areas of our lives to ourselves, a God-centered life surrenders the throne to Jesus. And when we live with Him at the center of everything, we can expect to live abundant, superior, and uncommon lives that lift us far above the mediocrity of ordinary, day-to-day living!

Responding to God's Word

God desires all of your life, not just a portion of it. Have you surrendered your life to Jesus Christ? Is He at the center of everything that you are and do? If not, what would be keeping you from doing that today? Spend some time making a list of obstacles that keep you from completely surrendering everything to Christ then take those things to Him in prayer!

DAY 2

With Our Whole Heart

"Teacher, which is the great commandment in the Law?" And He said to him, "'You shall love the Lord your God with all your heart, and with all your soul, and with all your mind. This is the great and foremost commandment."
—Matthew 22:36–38

Today's passage is actually a quote from the passage that we looked at yesterday. Jesus was approached by a religious leader of His day and asked a specific question. The question was, "Which is the greatest commandment in the Law?" Jesus's response illustrates beautifully what He desires for all of us. *"'You shall love the Lord your God with all your heart, and with all your soul, and with all your mind.' This is the great and foremost commandment."* Jesus took all of the law and summed it up, pointing to the most important thing that we could do. And what is this greatest of all commandments? It is loving God and not just loving Him, but doing so with *all* that we have. Let's consider the parts of our lives that should demonstrate this love for God.

First, we are to love God with all of our *heart*. The heart is the "seat of our affections." It is what we prioritize as being the most important to us. God tells us that the most important thing that we can do in this life is that of loving Him with our whole heart. That means that there are no areas of our lives that we keep to ourselves.

Loving God with our whole heart means that He takes center stage in all that we are and do.

Secondly, we are to love God with all of our *soul*. The soul is the portion of us that lives on into eternity. To love God with all of our soul is to love Him eternally. Yes, we love Him now, but that love and devotion carries on into heaven. If we really think about it, it only makes sense that those who love God now would be the same people in heaven for eternity. Only those who surrender their lives to Christ have eternal life, and without this spiritual transaction, we wouldn't love God or desire Him anyway.

Lastly, we are to love God with all of our *mind*. What we put into our minds should also reflect our devotion to God. It would be hard to make the argument that Jesus is the Lord and center of our lives while continuing to engage in everything that He opposes. That is why loving God with our thought life is as essential as the other two facets.

The point Jesus is making is easy to see. The most important thing that any of us could do is to love God. And this love is to be with our *whole* person. He doesn't just want one part of our lives but wants to guide us in every facet of earthly existence. "*All* of our heart, *all* of our soul, and *all* of our mind" makes it clear that He is to take precedence over everyone and everything else in our lives!

Responding to God's Word

Do you love God with all of your heart, soul, and mind? Are there areas of your life that you have kept to yourself, not allowing Him access? Make a list of those things and spend some time with Him today asking Him to be at the center of those areas too!

DAY 3

God's Support

For the eyes of the LORD move to and fro throughout the earth that
He may strongly support those whose heart is completely His.
—2 Chronicles 16:9a

Would you like to have God's strong support over your life? Today's passage tells us that God is willing to strongly support those whose heart is *completely* His. There are two words that stand out in this passage too important for us to ignore. One is that God is willing to *strongly* support people's lives. We could also say *fully* support. When God's favor is on someone's life, they are in need of nothing. Anytime we experience God's love, compassion, mercy, and grace in our lives, we are changed. It is almost indescribable what living in God's support and favor is like. But the reality is that God looks throughout the earth to fully and strongly support individuals.

But the second word is equally important. God will strongly support those who hearts are *completely* His. Notice that God's support, which is full support, can only be given to those whose heart has been completely surrendered to Him. Just like the other two passages that we have looked at so far, God is looking for those who will fully and completely give their lives to Him. He desires not a corner of our lives but the very center. He desires to bring healing, forgiveness, redemption, and purpose into every facet of our lives. But this only happens when He becomes the priority and we yield our whole heart to Him.

The New Testament is full of examples of what we can expect when we have the support of God. This support comes to those who have been born again and who have received the gift of God's Spirit. As Christians, we find the support of God through the amazing power of the Holy Spirit at work within us. Consider the following:

> Therefore we do not lose heart, but though our outer man is decaying, yet our inner man is being renewed day by day. (2 Corinthians 4:16)

One of the ways that we see God's support is through *spiritual renewal.* We are all aging, and while some people fight against that, the reality is that we are all getting physically older. But when we live with our heart fully surrendered to Christ, we find that although our bodies are aging, we enjoy spiritual vitality on the inside. Paul reminds us that this vitality is given to us *every day*! It is for this reason that we do not lose heart; rather, we have the necessary resources to continue on our journey. But once again, this spiritual reality is only for those who find themselves in Christ, fully positioned in the kingdom of God.

> Now to Him who is able to do far more abundantly beyond all that we ask or think, according to the power that works within us. (Ephesians 3:20)

As Christians, we also enjoy seeing God at work in our circumstances. God is able to do far more abundantly beyond anything we could ever ask or think. When we walk with the Lord, we will begin to see this become a reality in our lives. It is by the very power of God within us that we see Him doing "far more abundantly beyond." But this kind of living is also only reserved for those who have completely and wholeheartedly surrendered their lives to Christ.

> He who believes in Me, as the Scripture said, "From his innermost being will flow rivers of living water." (John 7:38)

Finally, we see Jesus describing what it is like to have God's power living within. When we *believe* in Jesus (which means trusting and surrendering our lives to Him), we will begin to see "rivers of living water" flowing from our lives. This is a word picture of what a Christian life should become. Everywhere we go, the power of God in us yields opportunities for us to expose people to "rivers of living water." Of course, Jesus is speaking of spiritual realities, things that the world does not and cannot accept. But for those of us whose hearts are completely Christ's, the full and strong support of God is ours to experience and enjoy!

Responding to God's Word

Is Christ on the throne of your heart? Do you love Him above all other things? Are you enjoying the strong and full support of God in your life? Would God say that your heart is completely His? If not, make a list of areas in which you need to surrender or resurrender to Him.

DAY 4

Priority to God's Kingdom

> But seek first His kingdom and His righteousness,
> and all these things will be added to you.
> —Matthew 6:33

What is it that you are seeking in this life? People may answer that question in many different ways but *fulfillment*, *purpose*, and *acceptance* seem to float to the top of most people's lists. In Christ, we find all three. And not just in small measure but rather, in Christ, we have *complete* fulfillment. In Christ, we have an *eternal* purpose. And in Christ, we find the *ultimate* in unconditional acceptance.

Our passage today is part of a larger portion of scripture in which Jesus is teaching us about our lives. Consider the following:

> Do not store up for yourselves treasures on earth, where moth and rust destroy, and where thieves break in and steal. But store up for yourselves treasures in heaven, where neither moth nor rust destroys, and where thieves do not break in or steal; for where your treasure is, there your heart will be also. (Matthew 6:19–21)

Jesus is actually dealing with material things and what our desires should be in response to "earthly treasure." Simply put, Jesus is telling us not to run after the things of the world; rather, we are to seek the things that are eternal. Does this require faith? Of course it does! He is instructing us to forsake what is seen in order to lay hold of that which is unseen. That is the very essence of faith. But in the latter portion of this passage, Jesus reminds us that the way in which we live our lives will ultimately demonstrate to whom or what we pledge our allegiance. Consider how He concludes the passage:

> Do not worry then, saying, 'What will we eat?' or 'What will we drink?' or 'What will we wear for clothing?' For the Gentiles eagerly seek all these things; for your heavenly Father knows that you need all these things. But seek first His kingdom and His righteousness, and all these things will be added to you. (Matthew 6:31–33)

Jesus is instructing us to not worry when it comes to the basic necessities of life. Rather, we should be seeking God's kingdom and God's righteousness as the priority of our lives. And what comes to a life that is seeking after the things of God? Jesus reminds us that the world seeks after all of the temporal things, yet God knows what we need before we even ask. Therefore, in Christ, not only will we find fulfillment, purpose, and acceptance, but Jesus tells us that God will take care of all of those temporal needs as well.

So the priority for people who do not compartmentalize their lives but rather make Christ the very center is that of seeking after the kingdom of God. And Jesus not only instructs us to seek God's kingdom but to seek it *first*. Again we see the Word of God emphasizing the importance of *total* surrender of our lives to Christ. In addition, we are to seek after God's righteousness, which is found only in Christ. The idea of righteousness is to be "right with God." But instead of trying to create this on our own through works or good deeds, as born-again believers in Jesus, we enjoy righteousness *credited* to us on the basis of faith. So seeking first God's kingdom and His righteousness means that we are prioritizing the kingdom of

God in our lives. Instead of building temporal kingdoms of our own, we find satisfaction in the things of God and of eternity!

Responding to God's Word

Are you seeking first the kingdom of God and His righteousness, or are you pursuing the same temporal things as that of the world? Do you find fulfillment, purpose, and acceptance in Christ or are you attempting to satisfy those needs by other means? Ask God today how you might prioritize or reprioritize the things that He values!

DAY 5

We Have to Make a Choice

No one can serve two masters; for either he will hate the one and love the other, or he will be devoted to one and despise the other. You cannot serve God and wealth.

—Matthew 6:24

"No one can serve two masters." Jesus's statement cuts at the heart of the notion that we can give Him only a portion of our lives yet still enjoy fellowship with Him. Perhaps compartmentalization is a way for us to feel good about our spiritual lives when all the while, we are really living for ourselves. In today's passage, Jesus states an eternal, spiritual truth that applies to all of us. We have to make a choice when it comes to living for Christ or living for ourselves.

If we examine closely what the world values and how it defines success, we will quickly discover that status, popularity, money, and power are all ways in which the world finds a sense of value and importance. Understanding this, Jesus goes right after the things that many build their lives around, namely material wealth or *mammon*. "You cannot serve God *and* wealth." The statement is concise and easy for anyone to understand. We have to make a choice.

Many people like the idea of heaven (some might not even believe there is such a place), but not many seem willing to let go of service to wealth in exchange for service to God. But that is exactly what Jesus is saying in this passage. We cannot do both. Either we will hate one and love the other or we will be devoted to one and despise the other. Jesus is making the point that devotion to money and the building of our own earthly kingdoms will yield a heart that is cold and apathetic toward the things of God. Of course, the opposite is true as well. Devotion to God and to the things of His kingdom will yield a heart that avoids the temptations and deception of earthly wealth. Everyone will find themselves in one of these two categories. We will either be devoted to Christ or we will be devoted to ourselves. Consider the following:

> But those who want to get rich fall into temptation and a snare and many foolish and harmful desires which plunge men into ruin and destruction. For the love of money is a root of all sorts of evil, and some by longing for it have wandered away from the faith and pierced themselves with many griefs. (1 Timothy 6:9–10)

Paul reminds us that those who want to get rich "fall into temptation." He doesn't say that they *might* fall but rather that they *do* fall. And with this aligning of our lives to the world's definition of success, we open ourselves up to all kinds of harmful and destructive lifestyles that bring ruin and destruction. The temptation for Christians might be to believe that materially wealthy people "have it all under control." But the truth is, if these same people are without Christ, they really possess nothing and will lose everything at the end of their earthly life. Paul goes on to say that because of this devotion to the building of an earthly kingdom, many had even wandered *away* from the faith. This makes sense and is in perfect harmony with what Jesus said in our passage today. Devotion to one means a rejection of the other. Jesus would reiterate the same truth in the parable of the sower. Consider the following:

> The seed which fell among the thorns, these are the ones who have heard, and as they go on their way they are choked with worries and riches and

pleasures of this life, and bring no fruit to maturity. (Luke 8:14)

Riches and pleasures are listed as the very things that will choke the spiritual life out of us. Of course, as believers, we know better, but the unbelieving world at large sees devotion to Christ over material things as nothing more than foolishness. So only one question remains: have you made your choice?

Responding to God's Word

Consider why God demands our devotion to Him as priority over all other things. Do you trust God to provide everything that you need in this life? Would you be willing to make life decisions based on what God desires rather than what you might believe is correct? If so, make that commitment to Him today!

DAY 6

The Things of the Spirit

For those who are according to the flesh set their
minds on the things of the flesh, but those who are
according to the Spirit, the things of the Spirit.

—Romans 8:5

When we put Christ at the center of our lives, effectively surrendering
to Him, we become people that care about the "things of the Spirit."
This cannot be said of the rest of the world. Today's passage reminds
us that there is a difference between the priorities of a redeemed soul
and one that has yet to be redeemed. For those who live according to
the flesh (worldly philosophies), the focus is on material things. Paul
reminds us, "For those who are according to the flesh set their minds
on the things of the flesh." This is quite natural because it requires a
movement of God in our spirit for spiritual transformation to occur.
Only when we come to Christ by faith do we begin to see things
through the eyes of God. This is something that an unredeemed soul
cannot do. Consider the following:

But a natural man does not accept the things of
the Spirit of God, for they are foolishness to him;
and he cannot understand them, because they are
spiritually appraised. (1 Corinthians 2:14)

A natural man is one that has yet to be saved. Paul reminds us that a natural man *does not* and *cannot* accept the things of the Spirit of God. He cannot understand them because they are spiritually appraised. For people who have not given their lives to Christ, religious knowledge may abound, but spiritual transformation and life has yet to take place. This person, in the natural state of being at enmity with God, believes the things of God to be "foolishness." And because it requires God's Spirit within us to change our hearts and minds, this natural man remains determined to live his life for earthly, temporal things.

On the contrary, Paul reminds us, "Those who are according to the Spirit, set their minds on the things of the Spirit." We know we are saved and possess eternal life when our priorities and desires begin to shift toward the things of the Spirit. Consider the following:

> But he who is spiritual appraises all things, yet he himself is appraised by no one. (1 Corinthians 2:15)

Born-again believers in Jesus Christ can begin to exercise discernment, effectively appraising the things that are happening in the culture. Yet the Christian is "appraised by no one" despite the persecution that can often come at the hands of those who consider the things of God foolishness.

There is a big difference between the priorities of someone who belongs to Christ and those who do not. Those who love the Lord with their whole heart and have surrendered their lives to Him will inevitably desire the things of God. These are things that are perfect, holy, and true. They are the things that will last throughout all eternity. But for those who have yet to receive salvation in Jesus, these are the ones whose priorities are set on earthly, temporal things.

Responding to God's Word

On what is your mind focused? Which statement best describes your life? Are you like those who are of the flesh or those who are of the Spirit? As you place Christ at the center of your life, receiving forgiveness and redemption, ask God to give you a heart for kingdom things!

DAY 7

Our Need for God

I am the vine, you are the branches; he who abides in Me and I in him, he bears much fruit, for apart from Me you can do nothing.
—John 15:5

If we are truly serious about living for the kingdom of God and making an impact on our culture with the gospel of Jesus Christ, we must keep Him at the center of our lives. Christ must be on the throne, and we must yield ourselves to His will. This is the essence of what abiding in Christ is all about.

In today's passage, Jesus instructs us on what is required for us to "bear fruit." There are many references in scripture comparing spiritual life to that of a healthy tree. Consider the following:

> How blessed is the man who does not walk in the counsel of the wicked, nor stand in the path of sinners, nor sit in the seat of scoffers! But his delight is in the law of the LORD, and in His law he meditates day and night. *He will be like a tree firmly planted by streams of water*, which yields its fruit in its season and its leaf does not wither; and in whatever he does, he prospers. (Psalm 1:1–3; emphasis mine)

> Blessed is the man who trusts in the LORD and whose trust is the LORD. For he will be *like a tree planted by the water*, that extends its roots by a stream and will not fear when the heat comes; but its leaves will be green, and it will not be anxious in a year of drought nor cease to yield fruit. (Jeremiah 17:7–8; emphasis mine)

Spiritual life is bearing fruit for the kingdom of God. Every born-again believer in Jesus has been given a gift or gifts that are to be used for the furthering of the kingdom. It's worth remembering that while the world is passing away, the kingdom of God is eternal. When we invest in His kingdom, we are investing in eternity and in the things that we get to enjoy forever. Not so with the world. Temporal things *will* pass away.

So Christians should be actively engaging in "fruit bearing." Like a healthy, green, and strong tree, we should be spiritually healthy and thriving, strengthened by the presence of God's Spirit within. As we abide in Christ, He promises to abide in us. And as we abide in Him, we begin to see kingdom fruit coming forth from our lives. Just as an apple tree produces apples and a pecan tree produces pecans, a transformed life, with Christ at the center, will yield spiritual fruit that will last forever and positively affect others.

This is why we need Jesus. Not just for the salvation of our souls but in order to do kingdom work, we must be yielded completely to Him. This is why Jesus says, "I am the vine, you are the branches." He supplies the power and ability for life-changing work to occur, but we must stay *in* Him. We must be connected to Him in order to see this kind of fruit from our lives.

Jesus finishes this statement by reminding us that apart from Him, "we can do nothing." Of course there are things in this life that we can accomplish, but for it to be eternal, spiritual, life-changing work, it only comes from a life completely surrendered to Jesus Christ!

Responding to God's Word

Now is a good time to consider whether you have compartmentalized God in your life or received Him as Lord and Savior. Only when He is top priority, above everyone and everything else, can we expect to see spiritual transformation. This is the essence of saving faith. Are you saved? Is heaven your home? Are you serious about following Christ, or have you just been playing games? He will come into your life today! All you have to do is ask!

CHARACTERISTIC #2

Trusting God

DAY 1

Faith Is Essential!

And without faith it is impossible to please Him, for
he who comes to God must believe that He is and
that He is a rewarder of those who seek Him.

—Hebrews 11:6

It really goes without saying; in order for us to place Christ at the center of our lives, we have to trust Him. At the very core of unbelief is an unwillingness to yield to or trust our lives into the hands of Jesus. Faith is essential! The Bible tells us that without it, it is *impossible* to please God. Have you ever wondered why that is?

For any earthly relationship to work, there has to be trust. Particularly in an intimate relationship such as marriage, trust is essential. When there is an absence of trust, there is no foundation left for which to build the relationship. That is why infidelity is so damaging. While broken marriages can find redemption and restoration, it becomes increasingly more difficult when one or both parties have been unfaithful.

So our relationship to God is the same. He loves us with an indescribable love. He has given us life. He has caused the penalty for our sin to fall onto Christ. God has done everything necessary for us to have uninterrupted, intimate fellowship with Him. Even when we were sinful, rebellious, and stubborn, He was making a way for us to be healed, restored, and redeemed. But in order to receive all of the benefits of a vibrant relationship with God, we must trust Him. We must rely on Him for everything. We have to put the world and its philosophies away and make room for the Word of God in our lives.

Today's passage tells us two things about faith. First, we must believe that He exists. When we look at unbelief, we often find those who rebel against the idea of God. Often this comes from a deep-seated desire to become God or at the very least to be the masters of our own lives. But the truth is that when we are saved, we move from unbelief to faith. We move from desiring to be in control to surrendering the control of our lives over to God. This will never take place without a willingness to trust Him.

Secondly, we are told that faith is not just in believing that God exists but also understanding that He rewards those who earnestly seek Him. Consider the following:

> Ask, and it will be given to you; seek, and you will find; knock, and it will be opened to you. For everyone who asks receives, and he who seeks finds, and to him who knocks it will be opened. If you then, being evil, know how to give good gifts to your children, how much more will your Father who is in heaven give what is good to those who ask Him! (Matthew 7:7–8, 11)

Jesus declares that everyone who asks receives. He tells us that everyone who seeks will find. And He proclaims that everyone who knocks that the door will be opened. These definitive statements, when united with faith, are quite powerful in the life of a believer. God desires to meet us where we are and to provide for us, physically and spiritually, everything that we need for the moment. And as we receive His provision, our faith grows stronger, and we move into an even deeper relationship with Him. This is particularly true of our prayer life. Consider Jesus's words:

> But you, when you pray, go into your inner room, close your door and pray to your Father who is in

secret, and your Father who sees *what is done* in
secret will reward you. (Matthew 6:6)

Again, we see the concept of being rewarded. Just as the writer
of Hebrews describes reward, so Jesus also promises that to all who
will quietly and privately spend time with Him.

Faith is essential, and that means that we trust God with *every-thing*. Not only do we make Him the center of our lives, but we also
rely on Him, trusting His wisdom and judgment. For us to live God-centered lives, faith is indeed essential!

Responding to God's Word

It is easy for us to say that we trust God, but are there specific
areas of your life in which faith becomes difficult? Write down those
areas, and take them to God in prayer today!

DAY 2

Salvation by Faith

For God so loved the world, that He gave His only begotten
Son, that whoever believes in Him shall not perish, but have
eternal life. For God did not send the Son into the world to
judge the world, but that the world might be saved through
Him. He who believes in Him is not judged; he who does
not believe has been judged already, because he has not
believed in the name of the only begotten Son of God.

—John 3:16–18

Today's passage contains three verses that have the power to change
the course of your life and your eternal destiny. Let's take a look at
each one and discover the life-changing power available to us when
we unite these truths with faith.

God's motivation for sending Jesus is *love*. In fact, God *is* love.
Known as *agape*, three words tend to surface when describing this
kind of perfect, godly love. The first is affection. This is God's *disposition* toward humanity. Because of God's incredible love for mankind,
He sent Jesus to become the perfect sacrifice for our sin. Secondly,
when describing love, we see goodwill. At the heart of goodwill is
the longing to see good things come to others. This is the *desire* of
God to see us come to salvation by faith in Christ and to find eternal
life. But finally, love without action is meaningless. So the last of
the descriptors for *agape* is benevolence. This is the willingness to *do*

something about the situation. God *gave* us His Son. God sent Jesus so that "whoever will believe" will not perish but have eternal life. "For God so loved the world, that He *gave…*" is a power statement. God was willing to do for us what we could not do for ourselves. God's motivation for sending Christ is love!

But the second verse is just as important. God's intention was not condemnation of the world but rather the salvation of the souls of mankind. He didn't send Jesus as a means of condemning the world. God's desire is that the world might be saved and that very salvation comes through Christ and Christ alone. When we place our faith in Jesus and what He has done for us on the cross, we experience spiritual transformation, and we move from spiritual death to spiritual life. That is the motivation behind worship. To give God the glory for who He is and for what He has done for us. Condemnation was not the reason why Jesus was sent but rather it is for our well-being, our salvation!

While the first verse gives us God's motivation for sending Jesus into the world and the second reveals His purpose, the last verse tells of the two groups of people that exist in the world today. There are believers and unbelievers. For believers (those who have been born again), there is spiritual life for the here and now as well as eternal life with God. For believers, there is no condemnation. Not so for unbelievers. Not only are we lost until we come to salvation in Christ, but we are also living in a state of being spiritually dead until that day. And if this condition goes unchecked, we lose out on eternal life and are eternally separated from God forever. This is not because some people are worse at sinning than others, for we have all broken the entire law of God. For the individual that does not have eternal life, it is simply because they have not *believed.*

This is what is at stake when it comes to the issue of faith. Not only do we need to trust God but that faith must be properly placed. Our hope is in what Jesus has done, not what we ourselves are doing. But with this faith comes a heart of gratitude. When we are saved, our attitudes, motives, and desires change. We now align our hearts with God and His desire rather than siding with the world. This is truly what it means to have been saved by grace through *faith*!

Responding to God's Word

Do you know that God loves you? Have you received salvation through faith in Christ? What would keep you from praying right now and asking Him to do just that? Why not take some time and ask God to give you the eternal life promised in this passage for all who would believe!

DAY 3

Praying in Faith

And Jesus answered saying to them, "Have faith in God. Truly I say to you, whoever says to this mountain, 'Be taken up and cast into the sea,' and does not doubt in his heart, but believes that what he says is going to happen, it will be granted him. Therefore I say to you, all things for which you pray and ask, believe that you have received them, and they will be granted you.

—Mark 11:22–24

One of the tremendous privileges that we have in Christ is total and complete access to the throne of God. As believers, not only can we have conversations with the Creator of the universe, but we are also encouraged to do just that. This is prayer, a never-ending conversation with our heavenly Father. God desires for us to talk to Him and to bring everything in our lives to Him. This includes thanksgiving for the things He has done, our victories, and yes, even our struggles. He wants it all and desires for us to trust Him with the most intimate portions of our lives. This is the essence of prayer.

Today's passage is a tremendous illustration of what God intends for our prayer life to be. Jesus begins with the declaration, "Have faith in God." One of the keys to a fulfilling prayer life is that of simply trusting God in everything. As believers, we understand that He has our best interests at heart. Even when He withholds what *we* think is best, we trust that He is providing for us and protecting us in all that we do. Faith in God is essential in order for us to enjoy intimate fellowship with Him.

But there is also a principle in this passage. When Jesus uses the phrase, "Truly, truly," He is announcing that the following words are eternal truth and that we can rest our entire existence on them. In this particular case, Jesus reveals that if we speak in faith without any doubting in our heart, that the thing in which we speak will be *granted* to us. This word *granted* is important because it reminds us that God is the one who determines what is best. But at the same time, we should never downplay the significance of what Jesus is teaching us in this passage. The spiritual principle is clear: faith-driven prayer *does* produce results!

There are two aspects to this kind of faith praying. One is that there cannot be *any* doubting in our hearts. This is easier said than done. We are often taught through life experience to expect disappointment. The truth is that people will often let us down. Because of our fallen humanity, there will be times when we will fail others, and they will fail us. But God is not subject to any of the fallen characteristics found in human nature; rather, He is perfect, righteous, and holy. And when He tells us that we should believe this principle of prayer, that is exactly what we should do. But the second aspect is equally important. Not only should there be no doubting in our hearts (for that would actually be questioning the very words of Jesus), but we should also believe in what we are speaking with our mouths. "Whoever *says*" and "believes that what he *says* is going to happen" are two key phrases in this spiritual principle. It is the speaking of God's truth that brings power to our prayer life. Praying in faith, believing what Jesus tells us, and not allowing anyone to convince us otherwise are elements to unlocking a powerful, faith-based prayer life.

Finally, Jesus applies this spiritual principle directly to prayer: "Therefore I say to you, all things for which you pray and ask, believe that you have received them, and they will be *granted* you." Again, we see the word *granted*. This is a reminder that God has the final word on answering prayer. But that is not to discount His desire to reward those who faithfully pray, believing in the very words that He speaks. Because of the principle of faith given, Jesus now applies that to "all things for which we pray and ask." God really does honor the prayers of those who believe Him and take Him at His word. And that is exactly how we, as believers, should approach the throne of God. "Have faith in God!" This is the heart within those who enjoy a dynamic, powerful prayer life!

Responding to God's Word

How would you describe your prayer life? Is it powerful, ordinary, or maybe nonexistent? How can today's passage lead you into a more satisfying time with God? Go to God in prayer today, and claim this spiritual principle over your life today!

A Portrait of Doubt

> But if any of you lacks wisdom, let him ask of God, who gives to all generously and without reproach, and it will be given to him. But he must ask in faith without any doubting, for the one who doubts is like the surf of the sea, driven and tossed by the wind. For that man ought not to expect that he will receive anything from the Lord, being a double-minded man, unstable in all his ways.
>
> —James 1:5–8

Today's passage is a continuation of what we learned yesterday about prayer. God is willing to meet us where we are and to bring wisdom into every situation of our lives. But asking Him for this wisdom, or anything else for that matter, requires faith. James reminds us that when we pray, we "must ask in faith." This goes far beyond just believing that God hears us. This strikes at the core of who we believe God to be. Asking in faith has everything to do with how we view the character and nature of God. The Bible gives us plenty of evidence that God not only desires to answer us but that He delights in doing so.

God gives generously to all, and He does so without reproach. This simply means that He will not scold us for asking. But just as James reminds us to ask in faith, he points out the result of praying with doubt. In fact, he gives us a portrait of doubt. The one who doubts as he prays is like "the surf of the sea, driven and tossed by the wind." Perhaps you have known someone who goes in and out of various philosophies attempting to answer life's questions. This person doesn't seem to stay with any one perspective too long but moves back and forth from one thing to another. This is not how we are to approach God. We come to Him with confidence, knowing that He loves us and has our best interest at heart. Rather than being "tossed around" by the world's philosophies and those who reject the Word of God, we place our trust in who God is and in His never-changing character and nature. We should pray, as James says, "Without *any* doubting." Again, this is easier said than done. Our faith can only be built in a relationship with Jesus. As we walk with Him throughout the years, our trust in Him should strengthen. And as we grow in our faith, we learn more and more about His amazing love, mercy, and grace. This realization assists us in removing doubt as we pray.

But James is not through painting this portrait of doubt. The man who prays with doubt in his heart "ought not to expect that he will receive anything from the Lord." Could this be the reason why some professing believers suffer in their prayer life while others thrive? It would seem so. Answer to pray is clearly made manifest through faith. Doubt is the obstacle that dries up our prayer life, causing us to become frustrated and disillusioned. For the man who doubts is "double-minded." In the original language, this means "two-souled." In other words, the person who doubts cannot decide who he is or what he believes. When we pray and ask of God while at the same time begin to wonder whether or not He will hear or even respond, we are exemplifying what it means to be "double-minded." This is not God's will for the believer. We are to pray in faith, believing in the very words that Jesus has spoken to us. When we couple faith in the Word of God with prayer, we avoid the mistake of mixing in doubt.

Finally, James reminds us that doubting demonstrates that we are "unstable" in all of our ways. If we were to hear that someone was mentally unstable, we would take that very seriously. But the same is true for spiritual instability. If we do not exercise faith in our prayer life, we demonstrate that we are just that, spiritually unstable. So by praying in faith, we are exercising our trust in God by relying on His character and nature. And this kind of praying will always yield results!

Responding to God's Word

Are there any characteristics found in today's passage that would describe your life? Take action today and ask God to assist you in removing whatever doubt might exist, ushering in a more vibrant personal time with your heavenly Father!

DAY 5

Mustard Seed Prayer

Then the disciples came to Jesus privately and said, "Why could we not drive it out?" And He said to them, "Because of the littleness of your faith; for truly I say to you, if you have faith the size of a mustard seed, you will say to this mountain, 'Move from here to there,' and it will move; and nothing will be impossible to you.

—Matthew 17:19–20

Desperation is the only way to describe it, the heart of a father toward his tormented son. This father had to watch demons attempt to destroy the boy. As the father got word of Jesus's disciples being nearby, he inquired of them to see if they could help. When that failed, he came to Jesus. Throwing himself at His feet, he pleaded for Jesus to intervene. Jesus did. The demons were cast out, and the boy was healed at once. We are not surprised at the powerful hand of Christ, but what do we make of the disciples' inability to help the boy? We might be tempted to conclude that Jesus did not give the disciples authority to cast out demons. But if we take that position, we would be in error. Consider the following:

> Jesus summoned His twelve disciples and gave them authority over unclean spirits, to cast them out, and to heal every kind of disease and every kind of sickness. (Matthew 10:1)

When we go back just a few chapters earlier in the Gospel of Matthew, we see that Jesus gave the disciples authority to cast out demons and even to heal "*every* kind of disease" and "*every* kind of sickness." So what was the problem? Why were the disciples unable to help this desperate father? Today's passage reveals the answer to those questions.

When asked directly why they were unable to exercise the authority already given them, Jesus points to the disciples' lack of faith. In fact, the original uses the word *unbelief.* It was their lack of faith that interrupted their authority. Consider the gravity of Jesus's statement. They had the authority, but it had to be united with faith in order for it to be made manifest.

Our faith in God doesn't have to be on a grand scale. In fact, Jesus says that if we have faith the size of a mustard seed (a very small seed) that we can "move mountains." Of course He is speaking in spiritual terms. But what if we applied that spiritual truth to our prayer life? Jesus is pointing to faith as a vital part of our spiritual lives. As we pray, we should pray believing, something we could call "mustard seed prayer." The more that we bring our lives before the throne of God and the more we exercise our trust in Him to respond from the heart of a loving Father, the more we begin to see His power at work in our lives. But Jesus doesn't limit the results of this kind of faith to just the "moving of mountains." Rather, He says that mustard seed faith can position us to discover that "nothing will be impossible."

So faith is essential in pleasing God. It is a vital component for the salvation of our souls. And faith, even if it is the size of a mustard seed, can bring about powerful results in our prayer lives!

Responding to God's Word

Have you allowed unbelief to limit the ability of God to work in your life? Would you describe your prayer life as one that is saturated in faith? Remember, mustard seed faith can "move mountains" and with it, Jesus says, "Nothing will be impossible." Thank Him today for His faithfulness to answer mustard seed faith!

DAY 6

Justified by Faith

Nevertheless knowing that a man is not justified by the
works of the Law but through faith in Christ Jesus, even we
have believed in Christ Jesus, so that we may be justified
by faith in Christ and not by the works of the Law; since
by the works of the Law no flesh will be justified.

—Galatians 2:16

Today's passage is a powerful one that reminds us that our justification before God is by *faith*. Often, we hear the age-old conversation dealing with the role that faith and works play in our spiritual lives. And while authentic salvation *does* lead to good works, the actual securing of our souls for eternity is done by properly placing our faith in what Christ has done for us on the cross. In fact, Paul tells us three times that justification is by faith while also reminding us three times that it is *not* by works.

First, let's consider the word *justification*. When we are justified before God, we are declared *righteous*. We are declared to be "as we ought to be." This can only come by faith because we are completely helpless to do anything that would make us right with God. Only when we admit our need and place our faith in what Christ has already done for us on the cross do we find ourselves justified. This is the beauty of the gospel. We cannot make ourselves right before

God but Jesus can. Consider Paul's statement pointing to faith as the means by which we are justified:

> Nevertheless knowing that a man is not justi-
> fied by the works of the Law but through *faith*
> in Christ Jesus, even we have *believed* in Christ
> Jesus, so that we may be justified by *faith* in
> Christ and not by the works of the Law; since by
> the works of the Law no flesh will be justified.
> (Galatians 2:16; emphasis mine)

And *remaining* in the knowledge that we are justified by faith is essential also. Because we fail in this life and because we have an enemy that brings accusations toward us, it is vital that we remember that our salvation and justification before a holy God is by faith and not works. Though we fail, we do not cease to remain justified. Because our salvation is secured by God, we can rest assured that we will see Him someday in heaven. Consider Paul's testimony regarding his own salvation:

> For I know whom I have believed and I am
> convinced that He is able to guard what I have
> entrusted to Him until that day. (2 Timothy
> 1:12)

But Paul also reminds us that works themselves, while an indication that salvation has occurred, plays no role in securing our justification. Consider the following:

> Nevertheless knowing that a man is *not justified*
> *by the works of the Law* but through faith in Christ
> Jesus, even we have believed in Christ Jesus, so
> that we may be justified by faith in Christ and
> *not by the works of the Law*; since *by the works of*
> *the Law no flesh will be justified.* (Galatians 2:16;
> emphasis mine)

To be *justified* is to be in right standing with God. This is why the gospel is superior to all other religious messages. All other religions require *effort*. Jesus calls us to *rest* in Him and the work that *He* has accomplished on our behalf as the means by which we are made right before God. Our justification before God is by faith! As Paul reminds us, "For we maintain that a man is justified by faith apart from works of the Law" (Romans 3:28).

Responding to God's Word

Have you placed your faith in the person of Jesus Christ? Do you know that you are justified? "For I know whom I have believed and I am convinced that He is able to guard what I have entrusted to Him until that day." Can you make that claim? Walk in the freedom and power of knowing that your salvation and justification have been accomplished by faith and not by works!

DAY 7

Righteousness Credited

For what does the Scripture say? "Abraham believed God, and it was credited to him as righteousness." Now to the one who works, his wage is not credited as a favor, but as what is due. But to the one who does not work, but believes in Him who justifies the ungodly, his faith is credited as righteousness, just as David also speaks of the blessing on the man to whom God credits righteousness apart from works: "Blessed are those whose lawless deeds have been forgiven, and whose sins have been covered. Blessed is the man whose sin the Lord will not take into account."

—Romans 4:3–8

Righteousness and justification are very similar. While we could find some differences between the two, they both carry the idea of being right with God. When we are justified before God, we are declared righteous in His sight. This is all done by faith in what Jesus has done for us on the cross. In today's passage, Paul uses two key scriptures to illustrate that our "being made right before God" is done only through faith in Christ.

The first of the two scriptures is found in Genesis: "Abraham believed God and it was credited to him as righteousness." As Christians, we, too, share in God's righteousness being applied or credited to our lives through faith in the finished work of Christ.

When we think of something being credited to us, we can think of a bank account. Someone comes along and deposits $10 million into your account. This money is given to you as a gift with no strings attached. You simply have to receive it and enjoy it. That is similar to what Christ has done for us spiritually. The difference is that we can earn our own money. But righteousness before cannot be earned; it must be received as a gift. This amazing, eternal, and life-changing gift can only be received by *believing* God and *trusting* in His promises. When we surrender our lives to Him, we find the righteousness of God *credited* to our spiritual account.

The second of the two passages comes from the Psalms. David also writes of salvation as coming apart from works. Consider the following:

> Blessed are those whose lawless deeds have been forgiven and whose sins have been covered. Blessed is the man whose sin the Lord will not take into account. (Psalm 32:1–2)

By faith, our sins have been *forgiven*. By faith, our sins have been *covered*. By faith, the Lord will not take our sin into account. In fact, the righteousness of God is now credited to our spiritual account. God can then view us as though we have never sinned. This is the definition of what it truly means to be blessed!

Paul uses these two scriptures to make the point that salvation and right standing with God comes through faith and not works. What we find in between the two passages from the Old Testament is a definitive look at how righteousness, forgiveness, and salvation occur in the life of a believer. Consider the following:

> Now to the one who works, his wage is not credited as a favor, but as what is due. But to the one who does not work, but *believes* in Him who justifies the ungodly, his *faith* is credited as righteousness. (Romans 4:4–5)

We don't work for our salvation. We receive our salvation through faith in the finished work of Christ. When we believe that God is willing to justify the ungodly (and that's every one of us), we are positioned to receive redemption. And when we properly place our faith in Christ, our faith brings about the righteousness that we could never secure in a lifetime of trying. So the key to finding salvation, righteousness, and justification is through faith in Jesus. And as we apply that same faith to our everyday lives, we find that we can live in a way that is pleasing to God, enjoying fellowship with Him, and seeing tremendous power in our prayer life. This is the power of faith!

Responding to God's Word

Are you trying to earn your way to heaven? Are you trying to do enough good things so that God will receive you? Remember, righteousness, forgiveness, and justification only come through faith in Jesus. If need be, rededicate your life to Christ today and walk in the power and freedom that comes through a life lived by faith!

CHARACTERISTIC #3

Spending Time with God

DAY 1

What's Done in Secret

But you, when you pray, go into your inner room, close
your door and pray to your Father who is in secret, and your
Father who sees what is done in secret will reward you.
—Matthew 6:6

It's the opposite of what the world would say. Things that are done in secret, in times when only God can see what is being done, are truly the most rewarding. The world believes that the loudest, wealthiest, and most visible people are the ones that make a difference. But God, in His infinite wisdom, has provided a way for us to experience His strength and power, enabling us to become those who make a real, eternal difference.

For some, it is referred to as a *quiet time*. But whatever we call it, Jesus invites us to spend time with Him privately away from all distractions. In today's passage, Jesus is giving us practical instructions on how to pray, not so much in *what* we say but rather in the logistics of what spending time with Him should look like. And to sum it up, we could use the word *secluded*.

Our world is full of distractions. For all of the good things that cell phones have brought into our world, it's not a stretch to suggest that they also bring with them a multitude of distractions. In fact, when we observe modern mankind in the cell phone age, we are likely to see people walking around with their heads down, looking at a screen. And mealtimes are often no exception. Even when spending time with people *in person*, many cannot resist the temptation to glance at the phone to see what the latest notification is all about. But no matter how technologically advanced our civilization becomes, a wise person will still take Jesus up on the offer to meet with Him in a secluded place.

"Go into your inner room, close your door and pray." These instructions lead us to a quiet place, a place where we can be alone with God. And this should be priority for every Christian given the busyness and volume of our current culture. Spending time with God is not only profitable for us, but it pleases Him. And as a result, we are empowered to move throughout our day with a proper perspective on what is all around us. And perhaps the most exciting part of Jesus's offer comes at the end of the passage. Jesus promises that for those who will spend quality time with Him every day, free from distraction, there will be reward. God sees the private and knows the thoughts and intent of our hearts. And for those who prioritize time spent with God, there is great reward!

Responding to God's Word

Are you currently spending time with God each day in a quiet setting, free from distractions? If you had to calculate the amount of time you spend on your phone versus that of spending time alone with God, what would that ratio look like? What adjustments do you need to make in order to spend quality time with God every day? Are you willing to make those adjustments?

DAY 2

Every Day Is a Gift

This is the day which the Lord has made;
let us rejoice and be glad in it.

—Psalm 118:24

Every day is a gift from God. How we begin our day will determine whether or not we are living a God-centered life. It is so easy to bounce out of bed, head for the shower, and move out into the world without the slightest thought of God or His desire for us in the day. But that is what the writer is telling us in this passage. Every day is handmade by God Himself. All of the potential to bring Him glory and to make an eternal difference in the lives of those around us is determined by how we begin the day.

And not only are we to acknowledge God *for* the day, but we are also to rejoice *in* it and express gratitude *for* it. There are always multitudes of ways to express our thanks to God for a brand-new day, but beginning each day with our minds and hearts focused on Him is a good way to start.

As the culture continues to swim in a sea of depravity and sin, we have the privilege of living on a higher plane. We are reminded that as the days get more evil, we are to live as those who are wise. Consider the following:

> Therefore be careful how you walk, not as unwise
> men but as wise, making the most of your time,
> because the days are evil. (Ephesians 5:15–16)

Living in godly wisdom is essential if we are to take full advantage of the opportunities to affect change for the kingdom. But unless we are beginning each day with hearts of gratitude and thankfulness, our day can quickly dwindle into just another day of chasing after the temporal things. Why not begin each day by acknowledging the Giver, giving thanks for the gift, and then launching out in a spirit of wisdom determined to make the most of our time!

Responding to God's Word

What is your focus when you wake each morning? Are you swallowed up in just trying to survive, or are you thriving in the truth that God has given you a brand-new day? What adjustments do you need to make in order to fully embrace each God-given opportunity?

DAY 3

God's Mercies New

This I recall to my mind, therefore I have hope. The LORD's lovingkindnesses indeed never cease, for His compassions never fail. They are new every morning; great is Your faithfulness.

—Lamentations 3:21–23

Christian hope is not like worldly hope. The world says, "I *hope* I get the job," "I *hope* my team wins today," or "I *hope* that the weather doesn't get too bad." All of these phrases ring with the sound of uncertainty. We might *not* get the job. Our team *might* lose the game. And the weather may *not* turn out the way we expected. But Christian hope is not like that at all. When Jeremiah proclaims, "This I recall to my mind, therefore I have hope," he is making a declaration of something that is sure and true. And what is it that he was recalling to mind? It is nothing less than that which should give each one of us tremendous hope.

First, we hope in the reality that God's loving-kindness indeed "never cease." If we break down that compound word, we see God's love and His kindness toward us. In Christ, God is able to pour out His amazing love and kindness on us because we trust in Him. Every new morning in which we wake is an opportunity for us to praise Him for His amazing love and kindness. But the word carries with it a deeper meaning as well. The compound word *loving-kindness* reveals God's nature of being a promise-keeping God. That's right!

God will always keep His promises. While we may fail to live up to everything that we promise, God's character and nature is one that delights in keeping His promises. And this character trait of God "never ceases." It doesn't grow old, get tired, or become worn out. And that is the very reason why we can have true, lasting hope in a dark world. Every morning, God's love, kindness, and faithfulness is on full display for anyone who takes the time to soak it up.

But secondly, God's compassion and mercy "never fails." Just like His faithfulness are His compassions and willingness to demonstrate mercy on all those who will trust in Christ. This certainly brings hope because we are depending on someone greater than ourselves. We are trusting in a loving God that has taken care of our sin in Christ. We can place our full assurance on His compassion and mercy because He is willing to pour it out on all who ask. This brings real hope into our lives as we bask in the glory of God's goodness and faithfulness. As born-again believers in Jesus Christ, we have reason to lay claim to God's mercy and grace. Regardless of what happened yesterday, last week, last month, or even years ago, we can start every day afresh with the forgiveness and grace of God!

Responding to God's Word

Can you say, with Jeremiah, that God's faithfulness fills your heart with hope? Are you soaking up God's love, kindness, compassion, and mercy afresh each new day? Spend some time today thanking Him for His love, which "never ceases," and His mercy, which "never fails!"

DAY 4

Draw Near to God

Draw near to God and He will draw near to you. Cleanse your
hands, you sinners; and purify your hearts, you double-minded.

—James 4:8

It's an invitation that goes out to each of us! Whether or not we take
God up on His offer is another matter entirely. James reminds us
that if we will "draw near to God," that God will "draw near to us."
Imagine not caring about drawing near to the Creator and the one
who loves us with an unconditional love. It's difficult to think about
a situation in which "drawing near to God" would not be considered
the wonderful offer that it most assuredly is. But if we are honest,
how many days pass in our lives in which we fail to draw near to
God? Yet the invitation continues to go out!

But there is more to this amazing passage. We are called to
"cleanse our hands" and "purify our hearts." This instruction works
on two different levels. First, "cleansing our hands" is to correct any
behaviors or actions that run contrary to the will of God. The work of
our hands is all that we do from day-to-day. As Christians, we should
desire to please God in all respects. In fact, we could argue that this is
the major difference between a life that has been redeemed and one
that has yet to undergo salvation. As those who have been bought
with a price, we celebrate, but not just over things that happen in our
lives here on earth; we rejoice in our eternal destiny, uninterrupted

fellowship with God Himself. So while we live these earthly lives, we want to please the one who died on our behalf. Grateful hearts produce lives that are in line with God's will and desire.

Secondly, we are to "purify our hearts." This deals with the spiritual side of our existence. Our thoughts, attitudes, desires, and motives should also be in line with God's desire. In fact, when we "purify our hearts," we are aligning our lives to be pleasing to God. It is only when our thoughts and attitudes are consistent with the Word of God that we can expect to live out those spiritual truths. As we draw near to God, we come to Him as we are. But the more we spend time with Him, the more we will see a transformation in our thoughts, attitudes, and actions.

Finally, aligning our lives to God's will is a way to avoid being "double-minded." The Bible describes those who attempt to hold on to the world and Christ at the same time as "double-minded." The primary reason for this is that we must, at some point, make a decision as to who or what will take priority in our lives. Either we will surrender our lives to Christ or we will continue to live as the rest of the world. Drawing near to God will assist us in making the right decision!

Responding to God's Word

Do you spend quality time with God each day? Are your actions, thoughts, attitudes, desires, and motives consistent with a life that is pleasing to God? Would God consider you "double-minded?" Make a plan today to draw near to God and enjoy His presence in your life!

DAY 5

Be Still!

Cease striving and know that I am God; I will be exalted
among the nations, I will be exalted in the earth.

—Psalm 46:10

One of the keys to spending time with God is to recognize busyness
and the role that it plays in distracting us from what is most important. It's not difficult to see all of the distractions in our lives today.
But we need to do more than identify these distractions. We need to
make a plan to schedule daily moments of simply "being still!"

That is the instruction that we see in today's passage. Staying
spiritually strong in a lost and sinful culture requires intentionality.
We must find the time to still our hearts and minds. We do this
by drawing near to God, giving Him the opportunity to speak to
our busy souls. The New American Standard Bible (NASB) trans-
lates this passage as "cease striving." This is God's will for our lives.
Consider the following:

> Come to Me, all who are weary and heavy-laden,
> and I will give you rest. Take My yoke upon you
> and learn from Me, for I am gentle and hum-
> ble in heart, and YOU WILL FIND REST FOR YOUR
> SOULS. For My yoke is easy and My burden is
> light. (Matthew 11:28–30)

God isn't demanding like what we see in the world. Jesus invites us to come to Him and experience rest for our souls. The more time that we spend fostering a relationship with God, the more we see His heart and find the capacity to really rest.

The Bible is full of instructions on "resting in the Lord." Understanding and enjoying the provision of God is another way in which we can "cease striving" and rest in His goodness. Consider the following:

> For this reason I say to you, do not be worried about your life, as to what you will eat or what you will drink; nor for your body, as to what you will put on. Is not life more than food, and the body more than clothing? Do not worry then, saying, 'What will we eat?' or 'What will we drink?' or 'What will we wear for clothing?' For the Gentiles eagerly seek all these things; for your heavenly Father knows that you need all these things. But seek first His kingdom and His righteousness, and all these things will be added to you. (Matthew 6:25, 31–33)

As Christians, we have every reason to "cease striving" while the rest of the world is anxious. The closer we are to our Savior, the more we are able to experience this spiritual rest. Listening to God by spending time with Him in His Word is essential in living a God-centered life, but it all begins with "being still."

Responding to God's Word

Is your life full of distractions? Are you fully invested in the things of eternity, or are you pursuing the things of the world? How we spend our time usually provides us with the evidence we need to honestly answer those questions. Make a plan today to "be still!"

DAY 6

God's Perfect Peace

The steadfast of mind You will keep in perfect
peace because he trusts in You.

—Isaiah 26:3

Perfect peace is the pursuit of just about everyone we will run into in this life. To live in a state of perfect peace is to enjoy a little slice of heaven here on earth. But this world doesn't promote peace; rather, it seems to dwell in the land of confusion, strife, and division. That is what makes today's passage so important. God will keep in perfect peace anyone who is "steadfast of mind." So what does it mean for us to be "steadfast in mind?" Steadfastness is the quality of being resolute. It is to live firmly and to be unwavering. And in what are we to be steadfast? We are to be unwavering in our faith and loyalty to God Himself. When we spend time with God, we are demonstrating, through our actions, the priority we are putting on our relationship with Him. And what is the promise for those who will live this kind of life? The promise is that God will keep that person in perfect peace, peace of mind, heart, and soul.

We see a similar promise in the New Testament as well. Consider the following:

Be anxious for nothing, but in everything by
prayer and supplication with thanksgiving let

your requests be made known to God. And the peace of God, which surpasses all comprehension, will guard your hearts and your minds in Christ Jesus. (Philippians 4:6–7)

Again, it is spending time with God that brings about this perfect peace. Paul says that we are to bring all of our requests to God. We are to spend time praising Him for the amazing things that He has done and worship Him simply for who He is. And as we spend time with God, bringing our requests to Him, thanking Him, and praising Him, the very peace of God will guard our hearts and our minds! Imagine someone standing at the door of your home, being vigilant to guard the possessions that you have within. Now consider Jesus acting as a guard over our hearts and our minds. Keeping out what doesn't belong and reinforcing that which is righteous, holy, and true. This is the result for anyone who will prioritize time spent with God. God's perfect peace surpasses all human comprehension and understanding, yet it becomes a reality for all who will come to Christ by faith and then live their lives in line with His desire and His will as revealed to us in scripture.

Responding to God's Word

Are you living in the perfect peace of God? If not, what things are causing you stress and anxiety? Would you be willing to take those things to God today and ask for His perfect peace? Spend time with Him today and experience the beauty and awe of His presence!

DAY 7

Focused on God's Presence

When I remember You on my bed, I meditate on You
in the night watches, for You have been my help, and
in the shadow of Your wings I sing for joy. My soul
clings to You; Your right hand upholds me.

—Psalm 63:6–8

How much of your day is spent focusing on the presence of God? In today's passage, David explains how focusing on the presence of God brought him hope, strength, and joy. The words *remember* and *meditate* are vitally important in understanding David's heart in relation to God. "When I *remember* you on my bed" demonstrates that David was solely focused on God whether he was going throughout his day or lying down in the middle of the night. "I *meditate* on You in the night watches" further indicates as to where David's mind was focused. What about us? Have you ever been awakened during the night or found yourself with an inability to sleep? What do you do with that time? For so many of us, it might be that we switch on the television or get on our phones. But David shows us a superior way to spend our sleepless nights. Focusing on God "in the night watches" brings our hearts and minds to a place in which we can relax and return to sleep. In fact, we see why this was true in the life of David.

First, David recalled the times in which God had been his help. As Christians, reflecting on God's faithfulness in the past always serves as a way for us to refocus our thoughts. It also promotes fresh faith and spiritual strength. God is indeed faithful, and reflecting on His track record in our lives is quite profitable for us, especially in times of trouble.

Secondly, David rested in "the shadow of God's wing." As he remembered God's faithfulness and meditated on God's goodness and provision, David was able to "sing for joy." Focusing on the presence of God enabled David to rejoice and gain new strength.

Finally, David writes, "My soul clings to you; Your right hand upholds me." Again, these are poetic references to the spiritual reality that God was trustworthy and that David could trust Him in every circumstance of his life. Focusing on the presence of God and spending time with Him daily will serve us as we seek to walk with Christ all the days of our lives!

Responding to God's Word

What about us? Do we practice focusing on God's presence daily, or do we go about our day without even a thought of His presence? Do we meditate on Him day and night? Is our relationship with Christ the most important thing that we have?

Go back through the last seven days of this devotional with others. Create a small group and encourage each other as you seek to prioritize your walk with Christ!

CHARACTERISTIC #4

Meditating on God's Word

DAY 1

Being Blessed

How blessed is the man who does not walk in the counsel of the
wicked, nor stand in the path of sinners, nor sit in the seat of
scoffers! But his delight is in the law of the Lord, and in His law
he meditates day and night. He will be like a tree firmly planted
by streams of water, which yields its fruit in its season and its
leaf does not wither; and in whatever he does, he prospers.

—Psalm 1:1–3

Do you want to be blessed by God? While most of us would probably answer that question with a resounding "Yes!", it is also likely that we misunderstand what true blessing looks like. We might only equate blessing with material things. And although God does bless us with material provision, it is the spiritual blessings that far outweigh the things that are merely temporal. In other words, it is possible for us to be materially wealthy and spiritually blessed. But not all blessed people are wealthy and not all wealthy are truly blessed. The acquisition of material wealth can be void of God's blessing. But when we see the activity of God in our lives and recognize it as *His* provision, both spiritually and materially, we find ourselves among those who can call themselves "truly blessed!"

Today's passage deals with what it means to be blessed of God. While this scripture gives us several things that a blessed individual will avoid, it is what lies at the heart of this passage that paves the way for receiving blessing upon blessing! Blessed is the man who "*delights* in the law of the Lord" and who "*meditates* on it day and night." At the center of receiving God's blessings is His Word. As Christians, we view everything in the Old Testament through the lens of the cross. We are no longer living under the old covenant. Rather, God has established a new covenant through His Son Jesus Christ. We are now justified through faith in Him. But with this justification comes a new desire, one for the very words of God. So this passage yields two important aspects to receiving the blessings of God, and both of them have to do with scripture.

First, we are blessed when we *delight* in God's Word. Consider the following:

> *Delight* yourself in the LORD; and He will give you the desires of your heart. (Psalm 37:4)

> Make me walk in the path of Your commandments, for I *delight* in it. (Psalm 119:35)

> Your words were found and I ate them, and Your words became for me a joy and the *delight* of my heart; for I have been called by Your name, O LORD God of hosts. (Jeremiah 15:16)

What does it mean to *delight* in God's Word? Let's consider what it means in every other area of our lives. When we delight in something, we like doing it. When we delight in something, we look forward to the next time that we get to participate in the activity. When we delight in something, no one has to twist our arm to do it. Just give us the opportunity, and we will be there because we delight in it. Now let's apply that to spending time in God's Word. Every time we open the Bible, we are giving God the chance to speak directly to us through His revealed and written Word. To delight in God's Word means that we take great pleasure in reading it, memorizing it, and meditating on it. To delight in God's Word means that we look forward to the next time that we can open it up and dive right in again.

To delight in God's Word means that no one has to twist our arm to participate in studying the Bible because we enjoy time spent there. When we prioritize time spent in the Word of God, we are making the best investment that we could possibly make!

Secondly, we are blessed when we *meditate* on God's Word. To meditate on something requires time. Meditating on God's Word goes beyond a mere cursory reading of it (although that is a good place to begin). When we meditate on Scripture, we are giving God the opportunity to pour over our hearts, minds, and souls His perfect will for our lives. As we spend time in the Bible, we begin to see things as God sees them. As Christians, when we couple God's Spirit with that of His Word, the pages of Scripture will begin to be illuminated for us. And this time spent with God in His Word will yield greater blessings than we could ever imagine.

But in today's passage, we see how this blessed man was meditating on God's Word. He was spending time in the Word "day and night." This is an indication that we cannot spend too much time in the Bible. In fact, many of us, in this busy world, may find it difficult to spend any time in the Word much less day and night; however, God's invitation still goes out to anyone who will prioritize spending time in His Word. And for that person, the blessings of God are many!

Responding to God's Word

Do you have a set time in which you spend time studying the Bible? How much time would that be as compared to doing other things (work, leisure activities, watching television)? Consider using this 40-day devotional as the means by which you get started on a consistent, daily adventure of spending time studying Scripture.

DAY 2

A Living Book

For the word of God is living and active and sharper than
any two-edged sword, and piercing as far as the division
of soul and spirit, of both joints and marrow, and able
to judge the thoughts and intentions of the heart.
—Hebrews 4:12

Mention the Bible and you will usually get two opposite reactions. Either people will run to the Bible, meditating on it and growing spiritually from it or you will have people that have nothing to do with it. Rarely do you find anyone in the middle. No other book brings about such emotion than the Bible. So why is that? Today's passage tells us why.

The Bible is not just a book. Rather, it is the very Word of God for mankind. God has given us the manual for life. In the Bible, sixty-six books from Genesis to Revelation, we find the answers to all of life's questions. The Bible tells us why we are here, it instructs us on our real problems, which is enmity with God, it tells us why we have this problem, and it even provides us with the solution. The Bible gives us guidance for daily living and warns us to avoid the pitfalls that can easily take us down. The Bible is eternal. The Bible is God's

Word, and those who are now a part of God's kingdom certainly recognize that fact. Consider what God has said about His Word:

> Heaven and earth will pass away, but My words
> will not pass away. (Matthew 24:35)

> The grass withers, the flower fades, but the word
> of our God stands forever. (Isaiah 40:8)

The Bible is eternal and will not pass away. The same cannot be said for the opinions of mankind. When we open the pages of Scripture, we are seeing into the heart and mind of God. When we see the person of Jesus Christ, as unfolded in the pages of Scripture, we see a Savior, the one whom God has sent to deliver us from our sin and to restore the relationship that He desires for us to have with Him. The Bible is more than a book; it is "living and active and sharper than any two-edged sword."

So why would anyone reject such a wonderful, living book? Perhaps the following verses of scripture can answer that question for us:

> For the word of the cross is foolishness to those
> who are perishing, but to us who are being saved
> it is the power of God. (1 Corinthians 1:18)

> But a natural man does not accept the things of
> the Spirit of God, for they are foolishness to him;
> and he cannot understand them, because they are
> spiritually appraised. (1 Corinthians 2:14)

Those who are perishing reject the Word of the cross because it is foolishness to them. When a person has yet to receive salvation in Jesus, they do not and cannot accept the things of the Spirit of God. So one reason for the rejection of Scripture is spiritual deadness. As much as we might not like to think about it, the reality is that rejection of God's Word is a rejection of God Himself.

Secondly, people may neglect the study of the Bible because they know that it might bring with it a conviction on their lifestyle. People living on their own terms will more than likely have this problem. Even those who verbally say that they do not believe the Bible could perhaps, in the back of their minds, understand the result of exposing themselves to such a living and active Word. Consider Jesus's words when discussing these people:

> This is the judgment, that the Light has come into the world, and men loved the darkness rather than the Light, for their deeds were evil. For everyone who does evil hates the Light, and does not come to the Light for fear that his deeds will be exposed. (John 3:19–20)

The simple truth is that many people know the truth about Jesus but like living on their own terms. Jesus says that these people will not come to the light, which is Christ, because it will expose them for who they are. Ironically, we are all sinners and coming into the light of Christ doesn't bring condemnation; rather, it brings healing, forgiveness, and restoration. And the wonderful news is that we are all invited to come to the light of Christ and receive spiritual life. And when we do, our attitude toward Scripture begins to shift. Instead of rejecting or neglecting this living and active Word of God, we are now drawn to it and love reading, studying, and meditating on it!

Responding to God's Word

So where are you? Do you daily expose yourself to the Bible and its contents? Are you growing spiritually in your walk and faith with Christ? Do you know others who are missing out on biblical instruction? How might you encourage them to daily feed on the Word of God?

DAY 3

Spiritual Transformation

Therefore I urge you, brethren, by the mercies of God, to present your bodies a living and holy sacrifice, acceptable to God, which is your spiritual service of worship. And do not be conformed to this world, but be transformed by the renewing of your mind, so that you may prove what the will of God is, that which is good and acceptable and perfect.

—Romans 12:1–2

One of the results of exposing ourselves to regular, biblical instruction is spiritual transformation. Today's passage instructs us on how the Bible can transform our thinking, our attitudes, and our lifestyle.

Paul begins by reminding us to present ourselves to God as a form of worship. This is at the heart of living a God-centered, Christ-centered life. We present ourselves to Him and yield to His will for our lives. The world would speak just the opposite. The world would have us believe that we should take control of our own lives, doing what we desire and want. But the Bible instructs us to do the opposite. Our posture before God is one of a servant. We understand that God does not treat us as such but rather He welcomes us into His kingdom as sons and daughters and fellow heirs. But our positioning before God is still one of humility.

Secondly, Paul instructs us to "not be *conformed* to this world." Consider the following:

> You adulteresses, do you not know that friendship with the world is hostility toward God? Therefore whoever wishes to be a friend of the world makes himself an enemy of God. (James 4:4)

> Do not love the world nor the things in the world. If anyone loves the world, the love of the Father is not in him. (1 John 2:15)

Living a God-centered life requires that we reject the ways of the world. We simply cannot hold on to both God and the world at the same time. At some point in everyone's life, a choice must be made. And that choice will affect not just the trajectory of our earthly life but will determine our eternal destiny as well.

Conforming is what the world would demand of us. When we think of conforming, we can think of making cookies. We roll out the dough and then use a mold to stamp out the various cookies, each one looking identical to the next. And when we live life differently as a result of our relationship with Christ, refusing to conform, the world will reject us as well. Consider the following:

> If the world hates you, you know that it has hated Me before *it hated* you. If you were of the world, the world would love its own; but because you are not of the world, but I chose you out of the world, because of this the world hates you. (John 15:18–19; emphasis mine)

> For the time already past is sufficient *for you* to have carried out the desire of the Gentiles, having pursued a course of sensuality, lusts, drunkenness, carousing, drinking parties and abominable idolatries. In *all* this, they are surprised that you

> do not run with *them* into the same excesses of dissipation, and they malign (insult) *you*. (1 Peter 4:3–4; emphasis mine)

Jesus makes it clear that the world will not like that we are not conforming to the same standard as they. Peter also reminds us that as we live God-centered lives, our attitudes and actions will not be the same as those of the world. When we live in a way that honors God, we will be insulted for it, and others around us will simply not understand why we don't do the same things as they.

But God has not called us to be conformed but rather we are to be *transformed*. Thirdly, Paul tells us that this transformation occurs when we are renewed "in our minds." This goes back to the idea of spending time meditating on God's Word. As we expose ourselves to the living and active Word of God, we are positioning ourselves to receive instruction, comfort, and even conviction from God by the power of His Spirit that lives inside of us. As we read, speak, memorize, meditate on, and believe the eternal Word of God, He begins to give us everything necessary for us to live out the truth (something we will discuss later in the book). As we yield to the power of God's Spirit that resides in every born-again believer in Christ, we see this transformation begin to take place in tangible ways in our lives. We then become less and less like the world and more and more like Christ. And this spiritual transformation is evidence that we are living God-centered lives.

Lastly, Paul tells us that as we renew our minds by spending time in the Word, we will be able to know what is the will of God. As Christians, we should not be wandering around like lost sheep unable to determine which direction we should go. Renewing our minds in the Bible and relying on the power of God will allow us to know what it is that God has called us to do and become. This is truly the most exciting and rewarding way to live, as we have been called to a higher way of living, rising above the usual and ordinary to experience the unusual and extraordinary and not just to exist but rather to thrive!

Responding to God's Word

Are you conformed to the world, or have you been spiritually transformed in Christ? Have you experienced rejection from others because of your commitment to Christ? Spend time today in God's Word, and ask Him to reveal to you His good, acceptable, and perfect will!

DAY 4

Diligence

Be diligent to present yourself approved to God as a workman who does not need to be ashamed, accurately handling the word of truth.
—2 Timothy 2:15

Diligence is persistence. It is a refusal to give up. Diligence is the tenacious pursuit of someone or something. Today's passage reminds us that as Christians, we are to be diligent in the study of God's Word. While Paul is writing this to a young pastor named Timothy, the study of the Bible is not exclusively for those who are in vocational ministry. Quite the contrary; the Bible is God's Word for us and is useful for teaching and training, rebuking and correcting (2 Timothy 3:16). The Bible is God breathed; therefore, we should spend as much time in it as we possibly can.

So what is Paul instructing us to do? We are to be diligent to "present ourselves approved to God." This brings forth an important point regarding our walk with Jesus. If we are to be sound in our doctrine and confident in our perspective on life, we need to base everything that we believe on the truth of God's Word. If we are not looking at life through the lens by which God views it, then we are setting ourselves up for failure. And spiritual failure is of far greater consequence than any other kind. But when we live according to the truth that God has provided, we begin to find ourselves living sound, stable, and confident lives in Christ.

Consider a life that is void of Scripture. If the person is an unbeliever, then this is nothing strange at all. Unbelievers reject the things of the Spirit of God. They consider them foolishness in that they are living according to the world and its philosophies (John 14:17). But for someone who professes saving faith in Jesus yet avoids Scripture, this would be an oxymoron. One of the characteristics of a life redeemed is the presence of the Holy Spirit living within the saved individual. And with the presence of God in our lives, there will naturally follow a desire to be in the presence of God and to learn from His Word. A rejection of the Bible is a rejection of God's instructions for our lives.

More practically, if we are not diligent in studying the Word of God, then how do we arrive at discerning what is true and what is not? The sad reality is that those who reject the Bible are attempting to build their own doctrines and philosophies, and if not corrected, those unbiblical beliefs will lead to their destruction. As Christians, we can avoid such things by being rooted and grounded in the truth given to us in the pages of Scripture. Paul reminds us that diligence in the study of God's Word will allow us to be "workmen" who need not be ashamed, knowing that we are "accurately handling the word of truth."

Diligence in the study of God's Word gives us a solid foundation in which to build our lives (Matthew 7:24–27). When we make meditating on God's Word a central part of our lives, we can be assured that we are seeing things through the eyes of God, allowing us to live in a way which is pleasing to Him (James 1:22). But perhaps most importantly, diligence in the study of God's Word reveals the true condition of our heart and demonstrates that we truly desire the things of God over that which is in the world!

Responding to God's Word

Do you make the study of Scripture a regular part of your week? Are you desiring more of God's Word as you continue your walk with Christ? Do you use the truth of the Bible in your day-to-day decision-making? Would you consider yourself a "workman who need not be ashamed, accurately handling the word of truth?"

DAY 5

Where Your Mind Is Focused

Therefore if you have been raised up with Christ, keep seeking the things above, where Christ is seated at the right hand of God. Set your mind on the things above, not on the things that are on earth.

—Colossians 3:1–2

What do you spend most of your time thinking about? Is it your work schedule? Perhaps it's the things that need to get done that day or that week. Maybe you like to dream and imagine what life could look like given a different set of circumstances. Today's passage reminds us that a God-centered, Christ-centered life is one that sets the mind on things above—eternal, heavenly things.

This passage begins with an "if." "*If* you have been raised up with Christ, keep seeking the things above." The assumption is that one must be saved, having undergone a spiritual transformation, before they will be interested in "things above." It seems that most people like the idea of heaven (some perhaps that do not even believe in its existence), but what Paul is referring to is *seeking* the things that are of God. We are not to sit under a tree somewhere and just stare up at the sky waiting for something to happen. Although as Christians we do get excited about the return of Christ, we are to be about the business to which He has called us. But as we live out our daily lives, we should acknowledge, with excitement, that we are moving toward eternity, and we should live with that reality in mind.

We are to "set our minds on the things which are above, not on the things that are on earth." This only makes sense for those who have surrendered their lives to Jesus and are living in a way that can only be described as *God centered*. But for those who are of the world, this is foolishness and nonsensical. It seems today that many are completely consumed with this life and the reward in which it brings. Without a regard for the things that are eternal, many seem to be living only for that which is temporal. But believers in Jesus are to be focused on God-centered, eternal things. So what does all of this have to do with meditating on God's Word? Time spent in studying Scripture allows us to refocus our minds from the busyness of this world and to prioritize the things of God over temporal pursuits. As our minds and hearts are strengthened through God's Word, we can then begin to order our lives around the pursuing of that which is better, greater, and eternal. This focus and pursuit of God's desires allows us to "make the most of our time" (Ephesians 5:16). And as we "store up for ourselves treasures in heaven" (Matthew 6:20), we begin investing in the most important thing that we could ever pursue—eternal life!

Therefore, if we have been raised up with Christ, enjoying a personal relationship with Him, we can begin living with eternity in mind. And even though we will have earthly things to do, we can prioritize the things of God and live out each day with "the things above" as our focus!

Responding to God's Word

Are you living your life with eternity in mind? Have you experienced salvation in Jesus? How much of your attention is put on "the things above?"

DAY 6

Delighting in God's Word

I will meditate on Your precepts and regard Your
ways. I shall delight in Your statutes;
I shall not forget Your word.

—Psalm 119:15–16

We need not neglect the Old Testament when studying the Word of God. In fact, some of the deepest, most heartfelt instructions for us come from this period in human history. Today's passage is a great example of what our hearts should be in regard to the Word of God.

First, we see once again the word *meditate*. The writer is demonstrating the proper attitude for us to adopt in regard to the amount of time spent in the Bible. To meditate is nothing short of a deep and meaningful pondering of the truth. In our world today, many believe that their schedule doesn't allow for even a cursory reading of Scripture, much less taking time to meditate on it. But the reality is that if we desire to see the hand of God at work in our lives, we must prioritize spending time in His Word. As we begin to read, speak, memorize, meditate, and believe on the Word of God, we begin to see things change. No, our circumstances may not change (although they certainly could). But even if they do not, meditating and believing on the Word of God will affect the most important change and that is change in our hearts.

Secondly, the writer mentions "regarding" the ways of God. A similar word that we could use would be *contemplate*. Now we are back to that of meditating. To meditate or contemplate means that we are spending the necessary time to absorb what is being presented to us. If we feel weakened in our walk with Christ, we need to check and see how much of our thinking is based on the world and its philosophies and how much of God's Word occupies our minds.

But thirdly, the writer uses perhaps the most important word, *delight*. We have already looked at what it means to delight in someone or something. When we delight in someone, we enjoy his/her company. We pursue various activities in which we delight because they bring us joy and fulfillment. No one has to twist our arm to spend time with someone that we like or to partake in an activity that we enjoy. Now compare that to spending time in God's Word. Do we delight in God's Word? Do we feel obligated to study it, or do we do so out of love and fellowship with God? This could easily be the most important word used in this passage because it represents the heart of the writer. When we have a heart for God, spending time with Him in His Word becomes second nature. We do so because we desire Him more than all other things!

Lastly, the writer says that he will "not forget" God's Word. The more time that we spend invested in the Bible, the more it becomes a part of us. And the more that it becomes a part of us, the more we can live according to the promises of God. Spiritual strength comes to those who regularly spend time with God and who make the study of Scripture a priority in their lives. We would do well to do the same!

Responding to God's Word

Do you delight in the study of God's Word? Are you living in the blessing of knowing Him personally? Are there any people or activities in your life that you have allowed to move in front of your commitment to live a God-centered life?

DAY 7

Faith Comes from Hearing

So faith comes from hearing, and hearing by the word of Christ.
—Romans 10:17

There are many reasons to immerse ourselves in Scripture, but if there was only one reason for meditating on the Word of God, it is found in today's passage. We are *saved* by faith (Romans 3:28). We are to *pray* in faith (Mark 11:24). And without faith, it is *impossible* to please God (Hebrews 11:6). So how do we obtain this faith that is so important for the God-centered, Christ-centered life?

Faith comes from *hearing*! Whenever the Word of God is spoken and heard, there is an opportunity for someone to respond to the truth. Conversely, it is difficult, if not impossible, for us to respond to something that we know nothing about. How many people must there be in the world who have never heard the gospel or the name of Jesus? This is why reading, studying, and believing Scripture is vital if we are to live a God-centered life.

Today's passage is the culmination of a larger portion of scripture dealing specifically with salvation. Paul reminds us that salvation of a human soul comes through *confessing* and *believing*. Consider the following:

> That if you *confess* with your mouth Jesus *as* Lord, and *believe* in your heart that God raised Him from the dead, you will be saved. (Romans 10:9)

Jesus has done everything necessary for our souls to be secured for an eternity with Him. Our response, however, is vital if we are to enjoy and experience His saving work in our lives. Paul reminds us that by confessing (publically) our reliance and faith in Jesus as the King of kings and the Lord of lords, we are bringing into our lives our very salvation. Offered by God's grace and secured at the cross, our salvation comes through confessing Jesus as Lord.

But coupled with our confession is the reality of our heart condition, which is that of faith *in* Jesus. By placing our faith in what is provided for us through the cross, we are positioning ourselves to participate in God's salvation for everyone who believes. And it is this faith in Christ that moves us into the position of righteousness before God. It is actually the righteousness of God applied or credited to our lives. Consider the next phrase of this passage:

> For with the heart a person believes, resulting in righteousness, and with the mouth he confesses, resulting in salvation. (Romans 10:10)

Our very salvation and righteousness comes through faith *in* and confessing *of* the name of Jesus. Paul goes on to remind us that this salvation is for anyone who will believe:

> For the Scripture says, "WHOEVER BELIEVES IN HIM WILL NOT BE DISAPPOINTED." For there is no distinction between Jew and Greek; for the same *Lord* is Lord of all, abounding in riches for all who call on Him; for "WHOEVER WILL CALL

> ON THE NAME OF THE LORD WILL BE SAVED."
> (Romans 10:11–13)

So how does one respond to the gospel if they have never heard? Well, the short answer is *they can't*. This reality is what Paul is referring to when he writes the following:

> How then will they call on Him in whom they have not believed? How will they believe in Him whom they have not heard? And how will they hear without a preacher? How will they preach unless they are sent? Just as it is written, "HOW BEAUTIFUL ARE THE FEET OF THOSE WHO BRING GOOD NEWS OF GOOD THINGS!" (Romans 10:14–15)

We are doing the greatest work on earth when we share the gospel with others. To see someone move from spiritual death to spiritual life is one of the most rewarding things of which we could ever be a part. But in order for saving faith to take place, the Word of God must be spoken; it must be declared. So faith comes from hearing and hearing by the Word of God! May we ever be diligent to read, speak, study, meditate on, and declare the written Word of God in order for our own spiritual growth to take place as well as for the propagating of the good news of Jesus Christ!

Responding to God's Word

Have you received salvation through faith in Jesus Christ? How are you participating in sharing the gospel with others? Decide today to make the study of God's Word top priority in your daily life!

CHARACTERISTIC #5

Living Out the Truth

DAY 1

Faith in Action

But prove yourselves doers of the word, and not
merely hearers who delude themselves.

—James 1:22

We've all heard the old adage, "Actions speak louder than words." And in the case of our spiritual lives, this is certainly true. As a rule, people don't want to know what we believe; rather, they watch how we behave. Today's passage is a good reminder that for professing believers in Jesus Christ, our actions have to match what we profess.

James points out that there are two kinds of people that come to the Word of God. There are those who hear God's Word and align their lives accordingly, and there are those who simply hear. Failure to live out the principles that we find in Scripture places us in a category of people who "delude themselves." We are living with a faulty view of the Christian life when we believe that we can hear the truth and yet not act on it.

There are some practical reasons why we are to be "doers of the word" and "not hearers only." First, it lends credibility to our message when we share the gospel with others. Our actions don't make the gospel of Jesus Christ true; that truth stands with or without our endorsement. But proper living validates, to the observer, that we have truly been changed by God.

Secondly, aligning our lives with the truth of Scripture enables us to grow closer to God. Consider the following:

> Submit therefore to God. Resist the devil and he will flee from you. Draw near to God and He will draw near to you. Cleanse your hands, you sinners; and purify your hearts, you double-minded. (James 4:7–8)

Yielding to the prompting of God's Spirit means that we can have an intimate, personal relationship with Him. By being doers of the word, we foster that kind of environment for our lives.

Lastly, as doers of the word, we position ourselves to enjoy everything that God has for us. When we fail to listen and follow His word, there is the potential for us to miss out on the best that God has for us. But by being obedient to the instructions found in Scripture, we not only protect ourselves from temptation but we have the spiritual power to move confidently as we live our lives for Him.

So how do we know that we are being "doers of the word"? First, we have to *know* His word. Neglecting to immerse ourselves in Scripture leads to spiritual ignorance, setting us up for believing things that simply are not true. So we need to *hear* the Word and that means spending time daily in study of the Bible. With that being said, how do we know that we are *doers*? Let's use the following passages as a means of assessing this:

> Ask, and it will be given to you; seek, and you will find; knock, and it will be opened to you. For everyone who asks receives, and he who seeks finds, and to him who knocks it will be opened. (Matthew 7:7–8)

> Therefore I say to you, all things for which you pray and ask, believe that you have received them, and they will be *granted* you. Whenever you stand praying, forgive, if you have anything

against anyone, so that your Father who is in heaven will also forgive you your transgressions. (Mark 11:24–25)

But I say to you who hear, love your enemies, do good to those who hate you, bless those who curse you, pray for those who mistreat you. (Luke 6:27–28)

In everything, therefore, treat people the same way you want them to treat you, for this is the Law and the Prophets. (Matthew 7:12)

These passages are a good place to begin but just scratch the surface in biblical instruction. We need to spend daily time in the Word so that we can clearly hear the voice of God and then we need to act on those instructions. And when we become "doers of the word," we can be assured that we are living a God-centered, God-pleasing life!

Responding to God's Word

Are you spending quality time in God's Word every day? Are you hiding His word in your heart? Would you consider yourself a doer of the word? Would you consider yourself a hearer?

DAY 2

A Solid Foundation

Therefore everyone who hears these words of Mine and acts on them, may be compared to a wise man who built his house on the rock. And the rain fell, and the floods came, and the winds blew and slammed against that house; and yet it did not fall, for it had been founded on the rock. Everyone who hears these words of Mine and does not act on them, will be like a foolish man who built his house on the sand. The rain fell, and the floods came, and the winds blew and slammed against that house; and it fell—and great was its fall.

—Matthew 7:24–27

There are two foundations in which each of us can build our lives. One is solid, dependable, and sure; the other is weak, fragile, and unstable. The decision is ours, but no knowledgeable builder would attempt to build floor by floor vertically without first securing a solid foundation. The same is true for our spiritual lives. Why would we ever attempt to work, save, and build our lives around anything but what is trusted and dependable?

In today's passage, Jesus tells us that the difference between the two foundations isn't rooted in whether or not we hear His words but rather the difference is found between those who act and those who ignore. Consider His first illustration:

> Therefore everyone who *hears* these words of Mine and *acts* on them, may be compared to a *wise* man who built his house on the *rock*. (Matthew 7:24)

First, the only way for us to *hear* the words of Christ is for us to spend quality time in His Word every day. Neglecting Bible study is easy to do yet doesn't position us to receive our spiritual nourishment. Not to mention that daily time in the Word keeps us from falling for false philosophies and the lies of the world. So in order for us to hear Jesus's Word, we have to read it, speak it, and meditate on it.

Secondly, we need to *act* on them. But in order for us to act on them, we need to value His instructions and trust that what He says is reliable. As we grow in our relationship with Christ, we begin to see that He brings to fulfillment in our lives the very truths in which He speaks. This brings spiritual life, victory, and freedom. So not only do we need to *hear* the words of Christ, but we also need to be proactive in *living* them out.

Thirdly, Jesus describes the person who hears His words and acts on them as being *wise*. Wisdom is quite different from intelligence. It is possible to be very learned in a particular subject even to the point in which people label you an *expert* in the field. These people might even be called on to lend their expertise and to offer advice regarding that particular subject matter. But intelligence doesn't equal wisdom. It is possible to advance in this life only to find that we are making bad decisions, particularly in our personal lives. Jesus is declaring the spiritual builder, the one who acts on His words, as one that is wise. Regardless of our level of intelligence, wisdom will always serve us well as we apply biblical truth to our lives.

Lastly, Jesus compares acting on His words to that of building our lives on the rock. Firm, reliable, and sure is the foundation of building our lives on Christ. In fact, to do otherwise is to forfeit this firm foundation. Consider what Jesus says about the one who fails to build on the rock:

> Everyone who *hears* these words of Mine and *does not act* on them, will be like a *foolish* man who built his house on the *sand*. The rain fell, and the floods came, and the winds blew and slammed against that house; and it fell—and great was its fall. (Matthew 7:26–27)

When we either fail to study the Word of God or simply ignore its instructions, we put ourselves in the category of the *foolish*. Living outside of Christ is equivalent to building our lives on sand. This unstable foundation will not hold up. The only true foundation in which to build our lives is the Savior Himself, the person of Jesus Christ!

Responding to God's Word

Have you surrendered your life to Christ? Are you living daily in His word and putting those things into practice? Are you living a God-centered life by putting Christ first, trusting Him, and spending time with Him each day? Why not begin today!

DAY 3

Evidence through Lifestyle

> But the seed in the good soil, these are the ones who
> have heard the word in an honest and good heart, and
> hold it fast, and bear fruit with perseverance.
>
> —Luke 8:15

Today's passage is another of Jesus's teachings regarding the importance of living out our faith. In this instance, Jesus is teaching the parable of the sower. He compares the preaching of the Word of God to that of sowing seed along the ground. Jesus describes four scenarios each illustrating a different heart condition. As the Word of God goes forth, everyone in the parable *hears* it. But only the last of the four kinds of responses describes a person who hears and puts into practice what they have heard. As a quick review of this parable, consider the following:

1. Response #1: The person who rejects the gospel

    > Those beside the road are those who have heard;
    > then the devil comes and takes away the word
    > from their heart, so that they will not believe and
    > be saved. (Luke 8:12)

For some, the gospel is never received. These people hear the Word, but they soon reject it. The devil snatches it away from their hearts so that they will not be believed and be saved.

2. Response #2: The person who fails to grow spiritually

Those on the rocky *soil are* those who, when they hear, receive the word with joy; and these have no *firm* root; they believe for a while, and in time of temptation fall away. (Luke 8:13)

These people hear the gospel and receive it with joy, but they never develop a spiritual root system. Therefore, when pressures come, they quickly fall away. Their faith is merely temporary.

3. Response #3: The person who gets caught up in the world

The *seed* which fell among the thorns, these are the ones who have heard, and as they go on their way they are choked with worries and riches and pleasures of *this* life, and bring no fruit to maturity. (Luke 8:14)

This third group is defined as those who hear, but the thorns of life choke out any spiritual life that they might have. The worries of life, the pursuit of wealth, and the desire for pleasures keep these people from growing in their faith in Christ.

4. Response #4: The person who has truly been transformed

But the *seed* in the good soil, these are the ones who have heard the word in an honest and good heart, and hold it fast, and bear fruit with perseverance. (Luke 8:15)

But it is the last group that demonstrates what it means to hear the Word of God, receive it, and hold it fast, living out the truths found in Scripture. All four groups *hear* the Word, but it is only those who *put it into practice* that Jesus deems "good soil." These are the ones who demonstrate that they have truly been transformed!

It is vital that our lifestyle matches the very truths found in God's Word. There must be physical evidence, displayed in our lives, that points others to the Savior. To live contrary to the Word of God demonstrates that we are not living wisely and that we lack understanding. Our lifestyle should be a living testimony to the reality that Christ is at the center of everything that we are and everything that we do. This is what it means to truly live a God-centered life!

Responding to God's Word

In the parable of the sower, which kind of soil best describes your life? Are you putting the truths of scripture into practice every day? Is there evidence, through your lifestyle, that you love the Lord and serve Him only?

DAY 4

Laying Aside the Old

That, in reference to your former manner of life, you lay aside the old self, which is being corrupted in accordance with the lusts of deceit, and that you be renewed in the spirit of your mind, and put on the new self, which in the likeness of God has been created in righteousness and holiness of the truth.

—Ephesians 4:22–24

Whenever we come to Christ by faith, we are changed, transformed, and saved. This new spiritual life that we find the minute that we are born again is nothing short of miraculous. It is only because of God's grace that we have the opportunity to call on His name and receive salvation. But it is by placing our faith in the completed work of Jesus that yields this salvation to us. The rest of our lives, after salvation, becomes a process of growing, maturing, and being strengthened in our daily walk with Christ.

Today's passage illustrates that when we are truly born again, we undergo a change in our attitudes, priorities, and motives. Instead of living for the world and its philosophies, we now desire to live in a way that is pleasing to God. That is what Paul is describing. Our lives before Christ were constantly being corrupted by desires and lusts. Whether that was material or physical, our former lives were all about us. Apart from Christ, we all live in a state of pleasing ourselves and living life "on our own terms." But the Bible describes this as being spiritually dead. We can pursue everything that this life has to offer and still have nothing. Only when we move from spiritual death to spiritual life do we really begin to live.

This is why Paul tells us to "lay aside the old self." He is referencing our *former* life before Christ. When we see the word *former*, we understand that at conversion, something happens to us on the inside. We now see our lives as the portion before knowing Jesus and the portion after we are saved. We are to die to our *former* self and lay it aside. Just like we would take off an old coat in order to put on a new one, we must shed our old way of living and adopt a new way, God's way.

So just as we lay aside the old, we are to "put on the new." Again, this means that our attitudes, priorities, and motives all begin to change. We no longer view this life in terms of how many years we might live. Rather, we view life through the lens of eternity. The things that we once counted as important now take a back seat to the things of God. Our minds are now focused on what is really important, and the priority now becomes our relationship to Jesus Christ.

What we find in between Paul's references to "laying aside the old" and "putting on the new" could arguably be thought of as the key to spiritual success. "Being renewed in the spirit of our minds" is what must take place if we want to experience joy, peace, and victory in our new lives in Christ. This goes back to the characteristics of a God-centered life. Making Christ the center, trusting Him in everything, spending time with Him daily, and meditating on His Word are all parts of the greater whole of renewing our minds. These principles are vital if we truly desire to move from our former lives to our new lives in Jesus.

Living out the truth means demonstrating that we have been changed and that this change has come from God Himself. Along with salvation comes the shedding of our old way of living and the adopting of a new way of thinking, one that is centered in the very Word of God. A new lifestyle speaks volumes on the new position that we now enjoy in our Savior, the person of Jesus Christ!

Responding to God's Word

Have you laid aside the old self of your former life before Christ? Are there any areas of your life that resemble the old? Are you willing to move away from these things in order to embrace the new?

DAY 5

Goodwill and Benevolence

What use is it, my brethren, if someone says he has faith but he has no works? Can that faith save him? If a brother or sister is without clothing and in need of daily food, and one of you says to them, "Go in peace, be warmed and be filled," and yet you do not give them what is necessary for their body, what use is that? Even so faith, if it has no works, is dead, being by itself.

—James 2:14–17

Today's passage gets down to the practical—what our faith should look like in this world. James holds nothing back as he unpacks the need for true faith to be demonstrated through action. It simply is not enough to say that we believe; we must live it out! So let's take a look at this important topic of being a people who are full of *goodwill* and *benevolence.*

Goodwill can be defined as "desiring good for others." When we have goodwill toward someone, we rejoice when they do well. When we consider the character and nature of God, we see this kind of goodwill. Jesus expresses it like this:

If you then, being evil, know how to give good gifts to your children, how much more will your Father who is in heaven give what is good to those who ask Him! (Matthew 7:11)

Because God desires to give what is good to those who ask, we, too, as believers, should be ready to do the same in the lives of those around us. Putting our faith into action means being full of goodwill and desiring to meet the needs of those in this world.

But what James is describing also includes the idea of being benevolent. Being benevolent means being willing to *do* something in a given situation. James puts it this way:

> If a brother or sister is without clothing and in
> need of daily food, and one of you says to them,
> 'Go in peace, be warmed and be filled,' and yet
> you do not give them what is necessary for their
> body, what use is that? (James 2:15–16)

Being benevolent goes hand in hand with goodwill. When we desire good for others, we then pair that desire with action. In other words, when we see a need, we are willing to meet the need in a tangible way. Again, we see God responding this way to the sin of mankind:

> For God so *loved* the world, that He *gave* His
> only begotten Son, that whoever believes in Him
> shall not perish, but have eternal life. (John 3:16)

God saw the need of mankind. He *loves* the world and because of that love He *gave* us Jesus. God's desire was for our good, and this moved Him to be benevolent by giving us Christ. And it is through Christ that we can be saved, forgiven, and redeemed.

Interestingly enough, two of the characteristics of *agape* (the highest form of love) are goodwill and benevolence. And because God *is* love, He personifies these two character traits. So James reminds us that if we claim to be *in* Christ, to be filled *with* His Spirit, and to be set apart from the rest of the world, faith and action must go hand in hand. It is when we are willing to meet the needs of others around us that we really begin to demonstrate our faith in Jesus!

Responding to God's Word

Are you living by faith in Jesus Christ? Does that faith yield tangible results in your life? Are you concerned with the needs of others around you, and are you willing to meet those needs as God leads?

DAY 6

Christid in Us

I have been crucified with Christ; and it is no longer I who live, but Christ lives in me; and the life which I now live in the flesh I live by faith in the Son of God, who loved me and gave Himself up for me.
—Galatians 2:20

Today's passage is a reminder that as Christians, we no longer live for ourselves but for the One who gave Himself for us. When Paul talks of being "crucified with Christ," he is not speaking of a literal crucifixion, but rather he is pointing to the reality that he has died to himself and has now surrendered his life over to the person of Jesus Christ. A big part of what it truly means to be a Christian is the willingness to get off of the throne of our lives and to allow that position to be occupied by Christ Himself. Consider Jesus's words:

> And He was saying to *them* all, "If anyone wishes
> to come after Me, he must deny himself, and take
> up his cross daily and follow Me." (Luke 9:23)

Although unpopular, if we are going to "follow Jesus," He has to be the one leading. This is difficult for anyone but especially those who desire to "run their own lives." But Jesus could not be any clearer; in order to be His disciple, we must "deny ourselves." This is the "being crucified with Christ" in which Paul refers.

Secondly, we no longer consider it to be our lives that we are living. Rather, it is Christ in us that is now our life. Paul says, "It is no longer I who live but Christ lives in me." To live out the truth in our lives, we first have to die to self and then be willing to be led by the Spirit of God, which resides in the life of every believer. We no longer just seek after our own desires, but rather we desire to please God in everything that we do. This is the essence of having "Christ in us."

Thirdly, Paul says, "The life which I now live in the flesh I live by faith in the Son of God." Yes, we still exist in human flesh and have to battle all of the things that come with that, such as temptation. But our strength is in our *faith*, and our hope is in *Christ*. Consider the following:

> Do you not know? Have you not heard? The Everlasting God, the LORD, the Creator of the ends of the earth does not become weary or tired. His understanding is inscrutable. He gives strength to the weary, and to *him who* lacks might He increases power. Though youths grow weary and tired, and vigorous young men stumble badly, yet those who wait for the LORD will gain new strength; they will mount up *with* wings like eagles, they will run and not get tired, they will walk and not become weary. (Isaiah 40:28–31)

This is the victory that we have when we place our faith in the person of Jesus Christ. We now have the ability to live abundant, uncommon, and powerful lives for the kingdom of God. But it all begins as we surrender ourselves to Christ, putting our desires away and taking on God's plan and desire for our lives. And why wouldn't we? God designed each one of us and is fully capable of guiding, protecting, and providing for us along life's journey.

Lastly, Paul gives us the reason why we should be so devoted to the person of Jesus: "He (Jesus) loved me and gave Himself up for me." It was Jesus who first gave Himself for our salvation. He led in showing the example of self-sacrifice for the benefit of another. We shouldn't do any less!

Responding to God's Word

Paul says, "It is no longer I who live, but Christ lives in me." Can you say the same about your life? Are there any areas that God may be asking you to surrender to Him today?

DAY 7

Living for God

> For the love of Christ controls us, having concluded this,
> that one died for all, therefore all died; and He died for all,
> so that they who live might no longer live for themselves,
> but for Him who died and rose again on their behalf.
> —2 Corinthians 5:14–15

The essence of being a Christ follower is that we live with the understanding that we owe everything to God. Therefore, we live in such a way that is pleasing to Him. In today's passage, Paul reminds us that as born-again believers in Jesus, we should "no longer live for [ourselves], but for Him who died and rose again on their behalf."

To conclude, let's consider some of the spiritual realities we enjoy as believers in Jesus Christ:

> This I recall to my mind, therefore I have hope.
> The Lord's lovingkindnesses indeed never cease,
> for His compassions never fail. *They* are new
> every morning;
>
> Great is Your faithfulness. (Lamentations 3:21–23)
>
> Bless the Lord, O my soul, and all that is within
> me, *bless* His holy name. Bless the Lord, O my

soul, and forget none of His benefits; who pardons all your iniquities, who heals all your diseases; who redeems your life from the pit, who crowns you with lovingkindness and compassion; who satisfies your years with good things, *so that* your youth is renewed like the eagle. (Psalm 103:1–5)

Ask, and it will be given to you; seek, and you will find; knock, and it will be opened to you. For everyone who asks receives, and he who seeks finds, and to him who knocks it will be opened. (Matthew 7:7–8)

Truly I say to you, whoever says to this mountain, 'Be taken up and cast into the sea,' and does not doubt in his heart, but believes that what he says is going to happen, it will be *granted* him. Therefore I say to you, all things for which you pray and ask, believe that you have received them, and they will be *granted* you. (Mark 11:23–24)

For He (God) rescued us from the domain of darkness, and transferred us to the kingdom of His beloved Son, in whom we have redemption, the forgiveness of sins. (Colossians 1:13–14)

This is just scratching the surface of the spiritual riches and promises that are ours in Christ. Because of God's great love, mercy, and grace, it's no great mystery as to why we should live out the truth in our everyday lives. After all, we should desire to bring others along with us!

And He said to them, "Go into all the world and preach the gospel to all creation. He who has believed and has been baptized shall be saved;

but he who has disbelieved shall be condemned." (Mark 16:15–16)

And Jesus came up and spoke to them, saying, "All authority has been given to Me in heaven and on earth. Go therefore and make disciples of all the nations, baptizing them in the name of the Father and the Son and the Holy Spirit, teaching them to observe all that I commanded you; and lo, I am with you always, even to the end of the age." (Matthew 28:18–20)

Responding to God's Word

How are you living for God? Are you participating in the spreading of the gospel? Are you growing in your faith? Make a fresh commitment today to live a God-centered life!

Moving Beyond the 40 Days

The ultimate goal of any Bible study or devotional should be two-fold. First, we should desire to move into a deeper relationship with God, and secondly, we should desire to live a lifestyle that reflects this intimacy. Below are some concluding thoughts that can assist you in moving even further in your walk with Jesus:

1. Our position in Christ

   Therefore there is now no condemnation for those who are in Christ Jesus. (Romans 8:1)

   It is vital that we understand who we are in Christ. We have a spiritual enemy, and he will look for opportunities to get us to question our position in Christ. But scripture is clear; if we belong to Jesus, there is now no condemnation for us to face. This is what we celebrate as believers!

2. Our invitation to intimacy

   But you, when you pray, go into your inner room, close your door and pray to your Father who is in secret, and your Father who sees *what is done* in secret will reward you. (Matthew 6:6)

   We should never neglect the daily invitation of spending time with God. Just like any other relationship, for intimacy to take place, we must spend time with the other person. Spending time with God daily brings the reward and blessing promised to us in scripture!

3. Our privilege to ask

Ask, and it will be given to you; seek, and you will find; knock, and it will be opened to you. For everyone who asks receives, and he who seeks finds, and to him who knocks it will be opened. If you then, being evil, know how to give good gifts to your children, how much more will your Father who is in heaven give what is good to those who ask Him! (Matthew 7:7–8, 11)

The statements that Jesus is making in this passage are definitive. It is not "you *might* receive," but rather it is "you *will* receive." We are given the direct instruction to ask of God, to seek God in everything, and to knock on the door of opportunity. When we realize how giving and good God really is, we begin to have more confidence in the asking. Not everyone has great parents but even for those who do, remember, God is better and more generous than any earthly parent!

4. Our adequacy to serve

Such confidence we have through Christ toward God. Not that we are adequate in ourselves to consider anything as *coming* from ourselves, but our adequacy is from God, who also made us adequate *as* servants of a new covenant, not of the letter but of the Spirit; for the letter kills, but the Spirit gives life. (2 Corinthians 3:4–6)

Our adequacy to serve God with our lives comes from Him. When we realize that we bring nothing to the table (except an availability and willingness), we are positioned to watch God do amazing things in our lives. We are ministers of the new covenant, of life in the Spirit of God, and that adequacy comes from Him!

5. The power of mustard seed faith

And He said to them, "Because of the littleness of your faith; for truly I say to you, if you have faith the size of a mustard seed, you will say to this mountain, 'Move from here to there,' and it will move; and nothing will be impossible to you." (Matthew 17:20)

Jesus tells us that even if our faith is only the size of a mustard seed, that same faith is able to move mountains. When we realize the importance of faith and how doubt and fear can keep us from God's best, we begin to understand how God responds to those who will completely trust in Him. The victory that we have *is* our faith in Jesus!

6. The power of mustard seed prayer

Truly I say to you, whoever says to this mountain, "Be taken up and cast into the sea," and does not doubt in his heart, but believes that what he says is going to happen, it will be *granted* him. Therefore I say to you, all things for which you pray and ask, believe that you have received them, and they will be *granted* you. (Mark 11:23–24)

This same mustard seed faith can be applied to our prayer life. We do not pray as a last resort nor are we to pray with doubt in our hearts. When we pray, we are to believe. This is Jesus's instruction to us, and His desire for His people. Mustard seed prayer yields amazing results because

God responds to those who pray in faith. We should take full advantage of Jesus's invitation for us to pray and believe!

7. The power of forgiveness

For if you forgive others for their transgressions, your heavenly Father will also forgive you. But if you do not forgive others, then your Father will not forgive your transgressions. (Matthew 6:14–15)

As we pray and exercise our faith, we must also forgive. Perhaps it's receiving forgiveness from God that we need. Maybe we need to forgive others or even ourselves. But there is no denying the fact that forgiveness has to be at the heart of a life of a follower of Christ. It might be difficult at times, but with God's Spirit at work within us, we must learn to forgive even those who might have hurt us greatly!

8. Evidence in how we treat others

And He (Jesus) said to him, "YOU SHALL LOVE THE LORD YOUR GOD WITH ALL YOUR HEART, AND WITH ALL YOUR SOUL, AND WITH ALL YOUR MIND." This is the great and foremost commandment. The second is like it, "YOU SHALL LOVE YOUR NEIGHBOR AS YOURSELF." On these two commandments depend the whole Law and the Prophets. (Matthew 22:37–40)

At the heart of all of this are the two commandments that Jesus gives, effectively summing up all of the law and Prophets. Loving God with our entire being (heart, soul, and mind) is the greatest commandment that we have. But the second is like it and it reveals how much we truly love God. We must love our neighbor as we do ourselves, and we must treat others the same way that we want them to treat us. These are not complicated commands, but they are necessary if we are to project an authenticity in our lives!

9. Responding differently than the world

But I say to you who hear, love your enemies, do good to those who hate you, bless those who curse you, pray for those who mistreat you. (Luke 6:27–28)

The true litmus test for our faith is how we react to life's challenges. We must react differently than the world reacts. Jesus tells us that we must *love* our enemies. He says that we are to do *good* to those who hate us. He instructs us to *bless* those who curse us and to *pray* for those who mistreat us. This is impossible in our flesh, but if we truly want to see Jesus displayed in our lives, this must become a reality. Success in these behaviors can only be found through the presence of God!

10. Grab hold of God's mercy every day

This I recall to my mind, therefore I have hope. The LORD's lovingkindnesses indeed never cease, for His compassions never fail. *They* are new every morning; Great is Your faithfulness. (Lamentations 3:21–23)

Regardless of what happened yesterday, last week, last year, or even decades ago, we are given brand-new mercies and opportunities every day. The only decision that we must make is whether or not we will walk in that mercy. Put the past behind you, receive His forgiveness, and press ahead toward the things which God has prepared for you!

About the Author

Dr. Steve Edge is a retired public educator from the state of Texas. He has pastored three churches and holds a master's degree in Christian education and a doctorate in educational ministry. Steve and his wife Diane are native Texans but like to spend time in the Colorado mountains as often as they can. It is their sincere desire that this book will assist you in your walk with Christ.